LOST TOWNS OF CENTRAL ALABAMA

PEGGY JACKSON WALLS

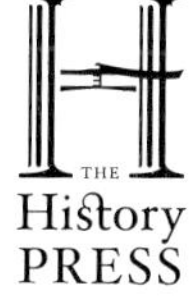

Published by The History Press
Charleston, SC
www.historypress.com

First published 2021

Manufactured in the United States

ISBN 9781467145190

Library of Congress Control Number: 2021937186

Dedicated to
Tyler, Tatum, Emma and Sophie.
Pursue your dreams wherever they may lead you.

CONTENTS

PREFACE

Every town has a story, even those that no longer appear on maps. Once thriving, well-populated communities became ghost towns when residents left their homes and moved to other places. The towns may no longer exist, but their stories remain. I regret I cannot include all the Central Alabama stories in this volume. Perhaps they will find a home in future books. The earliest stories return to Maliba, where, in 1540, Hernando de Soto arrived at the large, magnificent village. After enjoying the hospitality of the Natives, de Soto and his men attacked them and left the town in ruins. Chapter 1 of this book tells the stories of ancient Indian towns, Maliba, Tohopeka and Hillabee.

Other groups contributed to the history of Central Alabama, like the Coosa (Cosa) tribe and the tribe Aliambus, from which the state name *Alabama* is believed to have been derived. The word Alabama describes the Natives as "vegetable gatherers." In 1814, at the Battle of Horseshoe Bend, Andrew Jackson's militia and his allies won the decisive battle against the mighty Creek Nation. The federal government claimed the land and opened it to settlers. After Native Americans were removed to Oklahoma and settlers occupied the land, Indian names still identified creeks, rivers and towns as having once been their homes: Tallapoosa, Talisi, Wetumpka, Sylacauga, Hillabee and many others. Even while the Muskogee, Cherokee, Choctaw and other tribes were leaving, settlers, farmers and miners were arriving and establishing farming communities, mining camps, sawmills and blacksmith shops to service their needs. Stories about abandoned towns remain in the memory of people whose ancestors talked about drowned towns and textile towns. Older stories, such as those about early territorial and state capitals, are a part of Alabama history. Archaeologists, anthropologists and historians have unearthed remains of old towns, bones of ancient tribes, weapons and cooking vessels to determine how the people lived and how they died. Legends were born at Horseshoe Bend about heroes like Menawa, Sam Houston, John Ross and Andrew Jackson. In contrast, there were also Native Americans who betrayed their own people, such as Tecumseh and William Mcintosh.

Stories about ghost towns and the ghosts who live there are represented in Kathryn Windham Tucker's *13 Alabama Ghosts and Jeffrey* and *Alabama: One Big Front Porch.* The famous "Specter in the Maze at Cahaba" tells the story of Colonel Pegue, who died during the Civil War. Some people believe his ghost returned to his elegant home and gardens in Cahaba, Alabama's "most haunted town." Occasionally, visitors to the estate claim to have seen an orb moving about and following them as they walked in the garden. Windham's story suggests a ghost would be harmless unless he is disturbed by new inhabitants of his home. He may regard them as guests and not reveal himself, or he may regard them as intruders and disturb them with odd sounds or ghostly appearances, attempting to frighten them into leaving.[1]

The urban legend of Sloss Furnaces and Superintendent Wormwood describes the horrific lives and deaths of the men who lived in a nearby camp and worked at the furnaces. These stories, and many more, inspired me to write *Lost Towns of Central Alabama.* Please join me in exploring the old towns and learning about the people who lived there, where they came from and why they left.

ACKNOWLEDGEMENTS

Thanks first to my editor, Joseph Gartrell, whose patience with extended deadlines made completion of this book possible.

Literary friendships include Peggy Stelpflug, Carol Merritt, Bonnie Adams, Janell Kozak and Sandra Wilson, who accompanied me on presentations, workshops and research. Thanks to Kathyrn Braund for Native American resources and to Ralph Froshin Jr. for books and maps. For help with sources on coal mining in Jefferson County, thanks to Linda (Walls) and Tommy Tucker. Thanks to the Tallapoosee Historical Association for exhibiting my books at the museum in Dadeville; a note of appreciation to Danny Hayes, curator of the museum. I am honored to have my work represented among the treasured books and papers. Thanks to members of the Tohopeka chapter of the DAR and other lineage organizations for speaking invitations. To Tallapoosa publisher Kenneth Boone; Betsy Iller, managing editor of *Lake Martin Living*; and Kenny Dean, WAXCTV, thank you for reading and promoting my previous local history books, *Alabama Gold* and the pictorial history of *Alexander City*. Troy Jones, editor of OANews, shared his stories about growing up in the Union community, which was also partially covered with the waters of Lake Martin. News clippings, pictures, brief narratives and memorabilia of Union's history are available for viewing at the Tallapoosa Historical Museum. Thanks to Josh and Dylan Laminack, owners of the Fruithurst company in Cleburne County; to the B.B. Comer Memorial Library; to Shirley and Ted Spears; and to Ruth Beaumont Cook, author of *Sylacauga Marble*, for sharing your vast resources of pictures, stories and documents. Thanks especially to my sister Mary Williams, who listened to many stories before they were edited and written into *Lost Stories of Central Alabama*. Thanks for encouragement for this and other creative endeavors to my daughter Melissa Walls and my son Bill Walls.

FarmLinks and the Pursell family, Russell Lands and Robert Gunn were generous with their time, stories and photographs. Favorite resources include *The Encyclopedia of Alabama*, Alabama Department of History and Arts county histories and personal interviews with Central Alabama residents like J.C. Coley, Ralph Frohsin Jr., Thomas B. Saunders, Faye Luminack Hilburn and Barbara Cole, whose words made this book come alive with their stories.

INTRODUCTION

As I researched information about the ghost towns that were once home to hundreds, sometimes thousands, of people, I was guided by these questions: why were the towns established and why did they became ghost towns? The term *ghost towns* describes communities that were abandoned or those where little or nothing remains. Some, like Cahaba, were left with stories that support the claim of being an Alabama ghost town. The first towns were Indian villages and camps scattered along the creek sides and towns like Tohopeka, positioned in the toe of Horseshoe Bend and surrounded by the Tallapoosa River on all sides except for one. The first chapter in *Lost Towns of Central Alabama* tells the story of Native Americans who interacted with traders, settlers and explorers. Because only a few Native Americans could read or write English, they were at a disadvantage when treaties were written and laws were made. Andrew Jackson was viewed as a hero due to his military successes in the Indian Wars, especially in his victory against the Red Sticks in the Battle of Horseshoe Bend that destroyed the power of the great Creek Nation. His achievements ultimately catapulted him into the office of the presidency in 1828. Two years later, he created the Indian Removal Act and began what many viewed as the necessary removal of Indians from the white homestead sites. Rather than being forced from their land by federal soldiers, some Native Americans accepted the small amount of money offered to them by the government and left their villages voluntarily. Others remained and fought to keep their homes and ancestral lands. From 1836 to 1839, the federal military forced remaining tribes to march west to Oklahoma on what is known as the Trail of Tears. Many names of the Native American tribes remain and identify sites of their former homes and lands. Their stories have been well preserved and are the subject of extensive scholarly research, including accounts of the brutal Trail of Tears, on which thousands of Native Americans died. Former battlefield sites are now state and federal parks, with museums that preserve and display artifacts and illustrations of the first Americans' way of life.

Many Alabamians are surprised to learn gold mining was taking place in Central Alabama when settlers moved onto Native American land. Thousands of people rushed into areas like Goldville and Arbacoochee in the 1830s and '40s, when two gold rushes were taking place. Miners dug into the hard ground and soft soil from sunrise until the sun set in the west; then they worked at night by lantern light. However, when miners learned of the western gold rush, they abandoned their "diggings" in Alabama fields. They left on the same dirt roads they had followed into mining camps, leaving behind a scant history of Alabama's gold in the pocked hillsides and streams and in the names—Goldville, Goldhill, New Site, Old Susanna, the Devil's Backbone and hundreds of other sites.

Alabama's first capitals bustled with activity, including shops, inns, government buildings and brick streets. St. Stephens was the first territorial capital, and Cahaba (Cahawba) was the first state capital, followed by Huntsville, Tuscaloosa and finally the current capital city of Montgomery. A large part of Alabama's early history appears within the five different state capitals and the circumstances that created each.

Central Alabama had several mineral spring resorts, like Talladega Springs, that attracted patrons from as far away as New York City, Atlanta and Birmingham. The resort towns teemed with life and activities. People visited them to take advantage of the mineral water's health benefits. They arrived by the hundreds on the Louisville and Nashville Railroad each day to enjoy a luxurious meal and orchestra music. What happened to the fabulous resorts in Central Alabama and the people who visited them for treatment and recreation? Major events in the 1800s tell the story of the prosperous resorts and the subsequent downturn of Alabama's economic circumstances.

The Gantt marble mine, located near Sylacauga, has produced some of the world's finest marble. The white marble was used to construct the Lincoln Monument, the inside of the U.S. Supreme Court building and other notable places. What happened to Gantt village, where workers and their families lived? Is there still a market for Sylacauga marble?

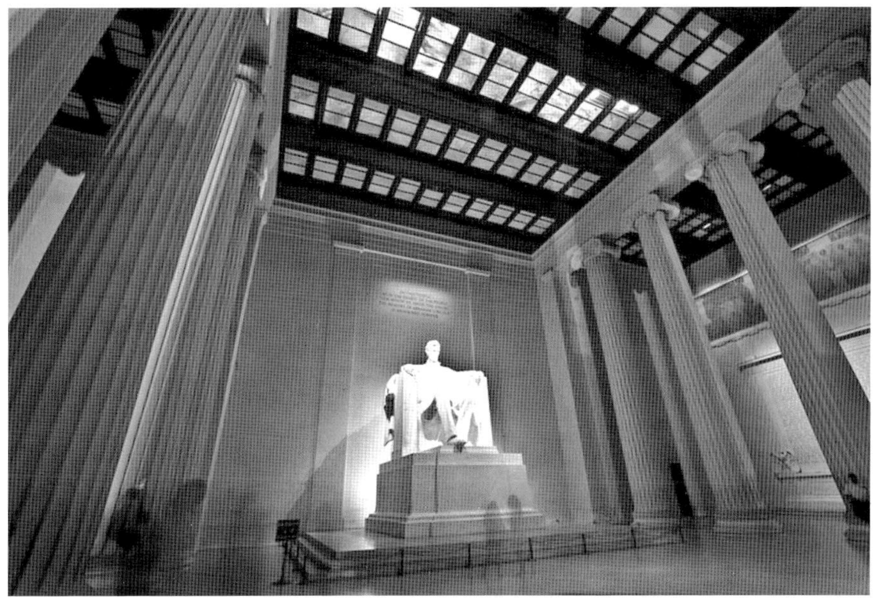

Gutzon Borglum used Sylacauga marble in making the bust of Abraham Lincoln prominently displayed in the United States Capitol rotunda. *Quarriesandbeyond.org/states/al/al-structures.html.*

Before starting construction on Martin Dam at Cherokee Bluffs, the Alabama Power Company constructed villages for the workers and their families, comparable to those in nearby Alexander City. How did the workers and their families live, and where did they go when the dam was completed and the water was released?

One of the towns partially submerged was Benson, an incorporated, all-Black town built by former slave John Benson. After emancipation in 1864, he worked in the Cahaba coal mines and saved enough money to purchase a piece of the land he worked on before emancipation. Over time, through hard work and frugal financial management, he managed to buy part of the farm. The story of Benson, the industrial school, turpentine business, churches and "lovely" homes has fallen between the pages of local and national history. *Lost Towns* shares the remarkable story of Benson.

In the latter part of the nineteenth and early twentieth centuries, cotton mills sprang up in southern towns. Avondale mills were scattered in small towns throughout Alabama and other states. Russell Mills in Alexander City provided employment for thousands of families and became internationally famous for Russell Sportswear. Both Russell and Avondale constructed mill villages for their workers, many of whom lived in the country and had limited resources for traveling to their jobs. Living in the mill village kept workers close enough to the plant that they could report to work on short notice if they were needed. In the early 1900s, child labor was common, but the jobs were dangerous and often involved tasks like climbing on machinery or working in small places adults could not enter. The children missed school each day and, as a result, had little education. Unions fought for laws that would limit child labor. After the Depression, union organizers attempted to enlist workers in unions. Often those attempts were met with violent resistance by management and, in some cases, by workers.

The town of Tallassee (Talisi) was given the name of the Native American tribe that once lived on the land. Tallassee was the oldest continuously operating mill in East Alabama, totaling 161 years. Like so many other plants, Tallassee mills burned to the ground.

Pepperell Mill in Opelika is famous for the movie *Norma Rae*, filmed in the village. Unlike many other mill villages, which burned or fell into disrepair, Pepperell remains well maintained, with the houses purchased by mill people or descendants and some investors in rental properties. Why did Pepperell and similar villages survive when others did not? What happened to the many mill villages where families lived and worked for the nearby textile mill? We'll look into that and more.

Chapter 1

ANCIENT INDIAN TOWNS

Mabila

In 1539, Hernando de Soto and more than six hundred Spanish soldiers laden with supplies came ashore near Tampa Bay, Florida. Their mission was to explore the interior of the southern wilderness and search for gold and silver. They entered Alabama from the northeast and destroyed Indian villages as they passed. In each village, they captured the chief and threatened to kill him if the Indians did not provide slaves, food and women. De Soto and his men traveled south by the east side of the Coosa River. The chroniclers recorded passing by numerous Indian villages on their way to Atahachi, Tuscaloosa's home. Tuscaloosa was a large, athletic and noble warrior who was an impressive seven feet tall. He sat on a large cushion and chair, on which Indians carried him to greet guests. His plumed headdress and cloak with feathers gave him the appearance of a mighty leader and one to be feared. Although Tuscaloosa was large, the conquistadors were able to take him prisoner. Tuscaloosa tricked de Soto by telling him he would lead him to the large town of Mabila, where he and his men could get bountiful supplies and captives. They arrived at Mabila on the morning of October 18, 1540, and found a large, well-fortified town with handsome houses. The town was surrounded by a fifteen-foot-high wall of tree trunks, cross timbers tied with large vines.

When Tuscaloosa commanded de Soto and his men to leave, they refused. A battle ensued that lasted all day. De Soto's chroniclers witnessed and recorded the bloody battle. Thousands of Indians reportedly were killed; only twenty-two Spanish soldiers died. Both Mabilans and the Spanish lost supplies and horses. The chroniclers described the town of Mabila in detail but omitted the location, which remains a mystery to the present day. Modern archaeologists continue to search for the ancient town of Mabila. Several times they have located a possible site and set up an excavation project to study bones and other relics unearthed in their digging. Albert Pickett believed the site "was upon the north bank of the Alabama, and at a place now called Choctaw Bluff, in the county of Clarke, about twenty-five miles above the confluence of the Alabama and Tombigby."[2] Pickett's conclusion was based on notes made by members of Hernando de Soto's party: Rodrigo Ranjel, de Soto's private secretary; and Luys Hernandez de Biedma, the commissary and the "Gentleman of Elavas." Noted scholar Charles Hudson presents another theory: "The general location for Mabila that fits most of the evidence now available is the vicinity of the lower Cahaba River. Mabila may, in fact, have been located at 'Old Cahawba,' the site of the first capital of Alabama. The capital was located at the mouth of the Cahaba River."[3]

The Indians resisted the attacks of the Spanish warriors, fighting valiantly for hours. Before the battle was over, thousands of Indians were killed or captured. During the battle, the conquistadors cut through the roofs of the houses for access to the Indians who fought from inside them. The final brutal acts of the Spanish were to set fire to the houses, take women prisoners and make slaves of the women and captured warriors. The Indians fought to the death rather than be captured and made slaves to the Spaniards. With no means of escape, some ended their lives by cutting the strings on their bows and using them to hang themselves inside a palisade.[4] Fernández de Biedma, King Carlos I's agent for the expedition, recorded in his journal, "We killed them all either with fire or the sword."[5] The conquistadors argued among themselves; some wanted to return to Spain, while others, including de Soto, wanted to continue their search for gold. When de Soto and the remainder of his party tramped farther inland, they found the great Mississippi River. By this time, de Soto was too ill to continue. He died beside the river he was credited with discovering. In three short years, de Soto and his party destroyed the lives of thousands of Native Americans and changed the future of those who survived their raids and slavery. "When the Europeans arrived carrying germs which thrived in dense, semi-urban populations, the indigenous people of the Americas were effectively doomed. They had never experienced measles

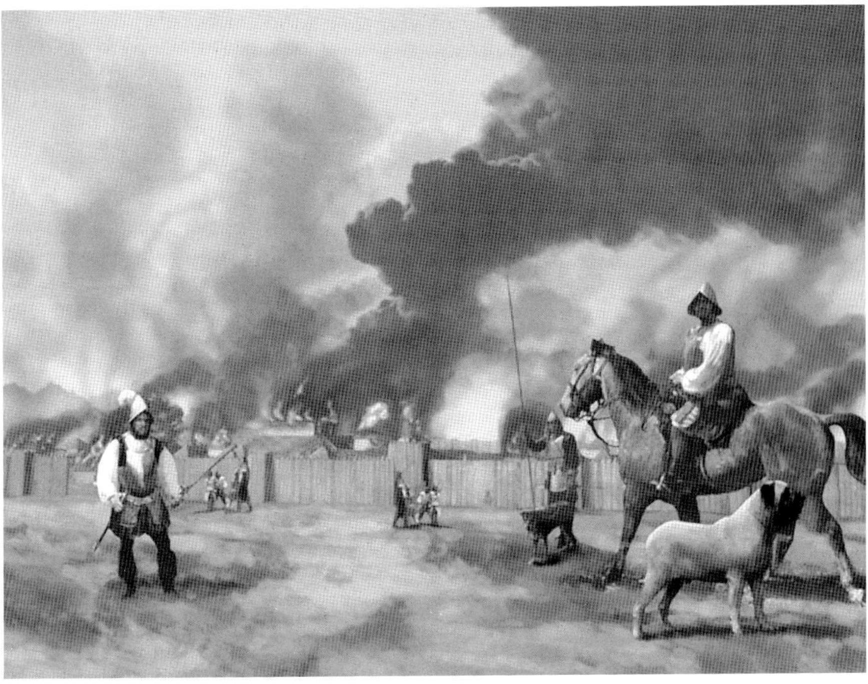

Hernando de Soto's men ravage and burn the large Indian city of Mabila, taking survivors as prisoners to serve as slaves. *Wikipedia.*

or flu before, and the virus tore through the continent, killing an estimated 90% of Native Americans."[6]

Albert Pickett described Mabila as the most important Indian town in Alabama in the mid-1500s. It is believed to also be the site of the bloodiest battle ever to take place on Alabama soil. De Soto's chroniclers witnessed and recorded the fierce battle between de Soto's conquistadors and the Indians. The Spaniards entered Alabama along the Coosa River and followed it to Talisi, which was most likely located near present-day Childersburg. According to historian Charles Hudson's widely accepted reconstruction of de Soto's route, they then headed west along the Alabama River.

The search for Mabila has interested many historians, including H.S. Halbert, Peter Hamilton and A.B. Moore, but no definitive consensus as to the location was ever made in their writing. The United States De Soto Commission was formed to determine the location of the site. It concluded Mabila was "probably somewhere in Southern Marengo County."[7] Although the commission submitted this conclusion to Congress in 1939, controversy regarding the exact location of Mabila continues.

In 1973, Dalton Smith, a supervisor for the Adams Lumber Company, discovered a large site some eight miles north of Choctaw Bluff, northwest of Gainstown and five miles from the Alabama River in south central Clarke County. After investigation, Dr. Walter B. Jones, former state geologist, did not agree, stating that Mabila was probably on the north side of Hal's Lake, covered with silt due to flooding in the area.

Tohopeka

Preparations for the Battle of Horseshoe Bend

Tohopeka was a temporary village, built by the Creek Indians to protect their families from Jackson's troops and allies at the Battle of Horseshoe Bend in what is now southeastern Tallapoosa County, Alabama. The Muskogee cut timber in the thick pine forest and built about three hundred log houses to protect 1,000 Red Stick warriors and 350 women and children. They created breastworks, a dirt-and-log barricade, across the narrowest point of the bend. The Tallapoosa River flowed on three sides, creating a peninsula where the Tohopeka Village stood. The Creeks placed their canoes at the toe of the Horseshoe Bend to be ready for escape. Indian people from the

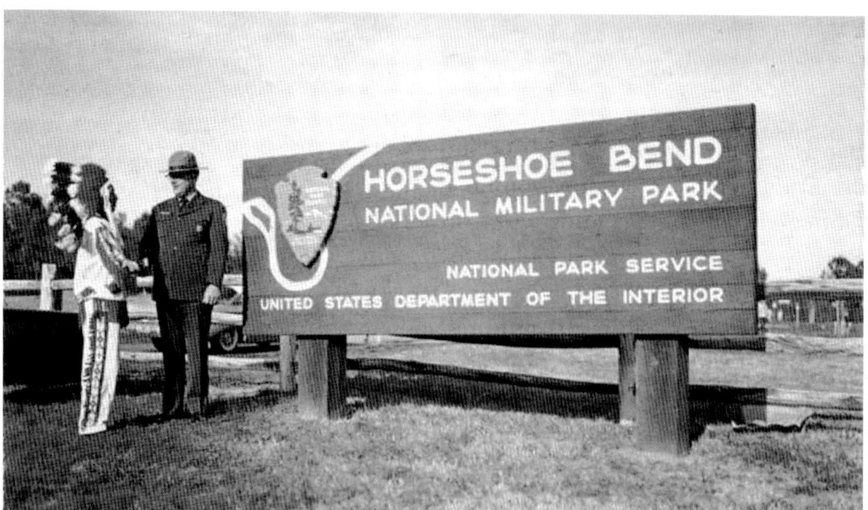

Horseshoe Bend National Military Park was established on July 25, 1956, the site of the last battle of the Creek War on March 27, 1814. *Courtesy of NPS.*

six upper Creek towns of Newyaucan, Oakfuskee, Oakchaya, Eufaula, Fishponds and Hillabee began moving to Horseshoe Bend for protection in December 1813. They continued to strengthen their defenses against Americans and to "fortify" Tohopeka against an imminent attack. The Red Sticks were prepared to fight to the death. Bitter experience taught them Americans did not want peace. They wanted the Creeks' ancestral land and would show no mercy to the Creeks until they possessed it.[8]

The Background

In the early 1800s, the Federal Road was widened for the passage of U.S. troops, horses and supplies. Muskogee Indians watched anxiously as federal troops rolled cannons and other equipment along the Federal Road onto their land. Settlers arrived with wagonloads of farming tools, weapons and supplies. Hogs, cows and other farm animals trailed behind or alongside them. As Creek Indians watched the influx of white families, protected by federal troops, tension increased each day. They were Upper Creeks, predominantly Red Stick warriors. The Lower Creeks, White Stick warriors, fought with the Americans against the Upper Creeks, federal troops, Cherokees and renegade Creeks. The White Stick warriors supported the Americans and joined them in raiding and destroying Indian villages.

The Battle of Talladega

In 1813, at Fort Lashley, the Battle of Talladega raged between General Coffee's Tennessee Militia and Menawa's Red Stick warriors. Two of the White Sticks who were captured and put into a stockade were Chief Chinnabee and his son Selocta. According to legend, Selocta escaped by putting a pigskin on his body with the pig's head fully attached. After dark, he grunted and rooted through the Red Sticks' camp. When safely away from the Red Sticks, he threw the skin aside and ran until he reached Jackson's camp at Fort

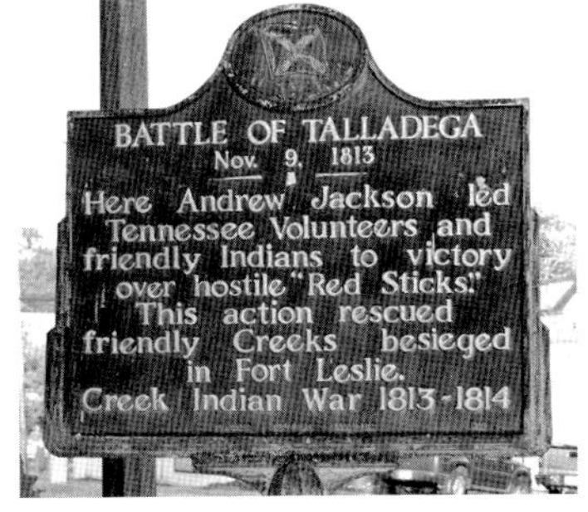

The Battle of Talladega was fought between the Tennessee Militia and the Red Stick Creek Indians near the city of Talladega. *AHA marker.*

Strother on the Coosa River. Jackson, with his men, rushed to Talladega and helped the White Sticks win a great victory. Legends like Selocta's tell how Indians used skin and furs to slip past their enemies. They were skilled in mimicking the sounds and behavior of animals and often employed them in tricking their enemy.[9]

The Canoe Fight

The following text appears on a marker erected by the Clarke County Historical Society in 2013:

> *On November 12, 1813, the Canoe Fight, one of the key assaults of the Creek War, took place nearby at the mouth of Randon's Creek where it flows into the Alabama River. Following the Fort Mims Massacre in August, small bands of Creek warriors persisted in attacks on settlements in the region. Capt. Sam Dale, stationed at Ft. Madison in Clarke County, volunteered to lead a mission to drive the Creeks from the area. The American militiamen, led by Dale, had launched their canoe the day before at Brazier's Landing (now French's Landing) and moved upriver where they encountered a canoe containing nine Indian warriors. The American militiamen were: Dale, Jeremiah Austill and James Smith. A ferryman named Caesar paddled the canoe and as the battle ensued, he held the two canoes together. One Indian was thrown into the water and the other eight were killed. As a result of this battle, the inroad of the Creek warriors on the west side of the Alabama River was checked and the settlers of Clarke County were able to return to their plantations and gather their crops and enlarge their improvements.*

Although the men had firearms, only Smith's gun fired. The river water dampened the others and rendered them useless. The Canoe Fight was not a major battle, but the skirmish between Mississippi Territory militiamen and Red Stick warriors was part of the Creek War. Captain Samuel Dale led the other men in the battle. Through his actions in the Canoe Fight, he became a hero and legend to the early Alabamians.

HILLABEE VILLAGE

Many Red Stick warriors at the Battle of Talladega were from the Hillabee towns, which stretched along Hillabee Creek and its tributaries in south Clay County and northeast Tallapoosa. The central village was Hillabee, which means "a stream ran through the area." The four satellite villages were Landushi Apala, near current Millerville; Echoseis Ligua; Oktasassi, near Alexander City; and Enitachopco of Bluff Springs. The mother village was Hillabee Town, near the Robert Grierson farm, where Grierson and his Indian wife, Sinnuggee, lived with their seven children: Catherine, David, Elizabeth, Liza, Sandy, Sarah and Walter. Grierson was of Scottish descent, a licensed trader and prosperous farmer. Sinnugge hired Indian women from nearby villages to work on the Grierson farm, growing vegetables and tending cotton fields. She paid the women with trinkets, glass beads and rum.

With an Indian wife, Robert Grierson was well respected by the tribes and traveled freely among them, buying and selling goods. The Griersons were also known and respected by white leaders like Benjamin Hawkins, the Indian agent for the Southeast. He was a frequent guest at what he called the "lovely Hilibis." Government officials like Marinus Willett and Indian leaders like William Weatherford met at the plantation to talk about economic matters, military maneuvers, Indian raids and treaties.[10]

Tensions increased between the Red Sticks, who wanted to keep the traditions of their ancestors, and those who were on the side of the U.S. military. In December 1813, Indian people from the six upper Creek towns of Newyaucan, Oakfuskee, Oakchaya, Eufaula, Fishponds and Hillabee began moving to Horseshoe Bend for protection, where they built the village of Tohopcka at the toe of Horseshoe Bend.

When war broke out in 1813, the Cherokees refused to join the faction of Creeks known as the Red Sticks, who were hostile to the United States. Instead, they fought alongside the Tennessee and U.S. troops under Andrew Jackson. Together they raided Creek villages along the Black Warrior River and fought in the November 1813 Battles of Tallushatchee and Talladega, from which they emerged victorious. Cherokee warriors played a major role in the attack on the Creeks of the Hillabee towns, who were members of the Red Stick faction. Following orders issued by Gen. John Cocke, the attacking party was unaware that the Hillabee tribes had recently surrendered to Jackson. This one-sided assault became known as the Hillabee Massacre.[11]

The Hillabee Massacre

When confronted with Jackson's troops and his superior weapons at Talladega, the Hillabee warriors decided to seek amnesty for their tribes. They asked Grierson to talk with Jackson and request a treaty. On November 17, 1813, Grierson went to Fort Jackson and offered the Red Stick flag to Jackson, asking for amnesty. After Jackson and Grierson reached agreement, Grierson left and started home to the Hillabees. At the same time, General White and his men were passing through the Hillabees to join Jackson for the Battle of Horseshoe Bend. Unaware of the amnesty, General White and members of his Tennessee Militia attacked the villages. They had no mercy on the Hillabee Indians, killing 64, wounding 29 and taking 237 as captives. The two satellite villages, Oakfusky and Genalga, also were destroyed.

"The other Hillabee towns, viewing this as flagrant treachery on the part of Jackson, became the most relentless enemies of the Americans, and afterwards fought them with fiendish desperation" at the Battle of Horseshoe Bend on March 17, 1814.[12]

The story of the "Hillabee Massacre" was told by Brigadier General James White in a report to his commander, Major General John Cocke:

> *We then proceeded to a town called Genalga, and burned the same consisting of 93 hourses.—thence we proceeded to Nitty Chaptoa* [Enitichopco] *consisting of about 25 houses, which I considered it most prudent not to destroy as it might possibly be of use at some future period. From thence we marched to the Hillibee town consisting of about 20 houses, adjoining which was Grayson's farm.*[13]

The Nashville *Whig* told the true story of the Hillabee Massacre on December 7, 1813, just three weeks later. The editor noted the deaths of sixty-four warriors. Another twenty-nine fell prisoner to the soldiers. The balance of the captives were women and children." The paper noted that eighty were African American. After explaining that none of White's soldiers were wounded, the editor continued: "It is scarcely necessary to add that none of our men were either killed or wounded,—when it is reported, that the enemy made no resistance whatever, except that they fired one gun.—They were literally butchered!"

The editor agonized over how men held in high regard could commit such an atrocity:

> [W]*e beg our readers to recollect, that this was the town which had only a day or two before sent in a flag to Gen. Jackson, assuring him that they would lay down their arms, and cease to war with us.—This was the reason they made no resistance. They will also recollect that Gen. White had not yet joined Gen. Jackson—was entirely ignorant of what had taken place; and had every reason to suppose that the enemy would conten*[d] *to the last moment. We know that General White would be one of the last men on earth, who would countenance such conduct.*[14]

The Day the River Ran Red

On the morning of March 27, 1814, the Battle of Horseshoe Bend began. Jackson and his men got into position to attack the Red Sticks, who stood ready to defend their ancestral lands. Creek Chief Menawa tried to dissuade the Creeks from waging war with the Americans. Finally, seeing he could not change their minds, he led the Red Stick warriors into battle. After the fighting began, Menawa and the medicine man disagreed on the tactics they would use. The prophet had a great following among the Creeks, but when Menawa slayed him on the spot, the Red Sticks followed Menawa's directions. From the beginning, the odds were against the Indians. Jackson's 3,300 men included 500 Cherokee and 100 Lower Creek White Stick warriors. On the other side, the Red Sticks numbered about 1,000 warriors. Only a third of the men who were defending the barricade possessed a musket or rifle. The barricade effectively held the soldiers back for two hours as they fired on the wall. The Red Sticks watched, waiting for a hand-to-hand battle. Making a decisive move, Jackson ordered the soldiers to blow a hole in the wall with a cannon. The American troops then entered through the opening to fight the Red Sticks. "Meanwhile, across the river from Tohopeka, three of Coffee's Cherokee warriors slipped into the river and swam to canoes lying on the opposite bank. Using the stolen canoes, the Cherokee and Lower Creek warriors crossed the river in increasing numbers, attacking, and burning Tohopeka from the rear."[15]

At the end of the day, 49 of Jackson's troops were killed and 154 wounded. About 300 Red Sticks who attempted to swim to the canoes were shot in the water. More than 800 Red Sticks were killed that day. The remaining 350 Upper Creek women and children were made prisoners of the Cherokee and Lower Creek warriors. On that date, March 27, 1814, the power of the

Great Creek Nation was lost and would never be regained. The Tallapoosa County River ran red with Creek blood.

On August 9, 1814, Jackson and Creek chiefs signed the Treaty of Fort Jackson. The treaty ended the Creek War and gave the United States approximately twenty-three million acres of Creek land. Most of the land officially became the state of Alabama in 1819.[16]

Why the Creeks Did Not Surrender

At the Battle of Horseshoe Bend, when the outcome of the battle was assured and Indians were being slaughtered by the superior weapons and numbers of Americans and Cherokee, Andrew Jackson twice sent a courier to Weatherford (Menawa) to offer the Red Sticks a chance to surrender. They felt Jackson had betrayed them after agreeing to amnesty for the Hillabee tribes and did not trust his word. They believed Jackson allowed the Tennessee Militia to attack and destroy their villages. Another reason the Red Sticks did not surrender was the assurance of a Shawnee prophet that they would be safe. The prophet promised the Red Sticks the Great Spirit would protect them from the bullets of their enemies and no weapon could harm them. The Shawnee prophet's lie contributed to hundreds of the Creek warriors' deaths.

Legendary Heroes at Horseshoe Bend

Menawa's brave exploits and survival at the Battle of Horseshoe Bend were told in two different versions of events. The first story told how he was shot seven times and lay among the dead until darkness fell. Then he dragged himself to the river and lay in a canoe as it drifted downstream to where Indian women were hiding. They saw the canoe, pulled it ashore and cared for Menawa until he was healed. The brave warrior then rode to Fort Jackson to surrender. General Jackson and his men must have thought they were looking at the ghost of Menawa. Startled, a soldier moved to kill Menawa. Jackson stopped him, saying, "You would cheat death of such a brave man."[17]

A second story describes Menawa's escape:

> *He jumped into the water and holding to a root, he breathed through a cane he held in his mouth and the other end protruding above the surface.*

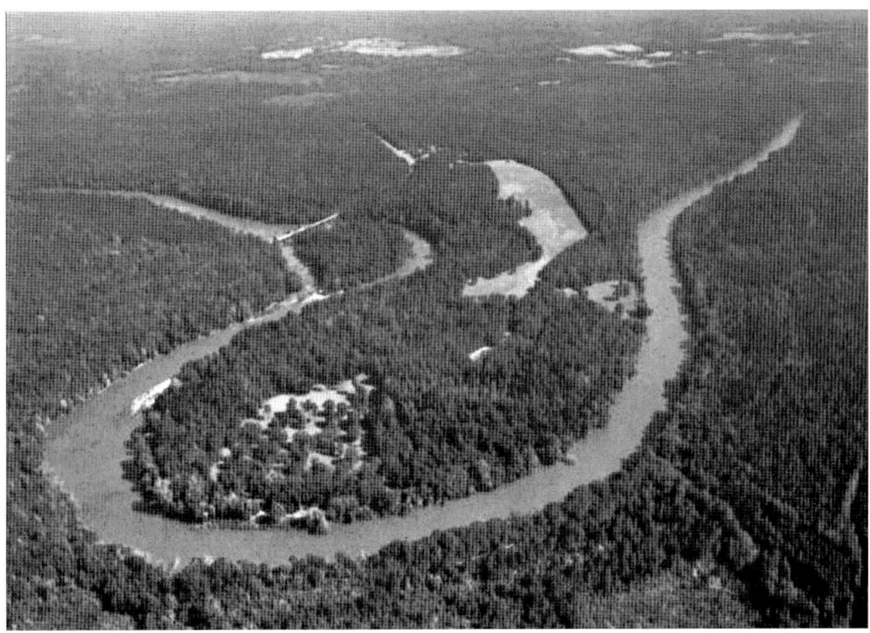

The Tohopeka Village was located in the toe of Horseshoe Bend, where Andrew Jackson and his militia defeated the Red Sticks and their allies. *Courtesy of NPS.*

> *Under the cover of night, he escaped into the woods, grievously wounded. Years later, Picket spoke with Menawa, who told him how he made his escape. "His face, limbs and body, at the time we conversed with him were marked with the scars of many horrible wounds. Another Chief was shot down, among a number of slain warriors, and, with admirable presence of mind, saved his life by drawing over him the bodies of two of them under which he lay, till the darkness of night permitted him to leave the horrible place.*[18]

Menawa was also known as "Red Eagle." Impressed by the story of Red Eagle's escape from pursuing enemies, Alexander V. Meek published his most ambitious work in 1855, a book-length narrative poem, *The Red Eagle: A Poem of the South*, set during the Creek War of 1813–14. The narrative poem about Creek Chief William Weatherford (Menawa, "Red Eagle") centers on the events of the Creek War. The narrative begins with the massacre at Fort Mims on August 30, 1813, and ends with Weatherford's surrender to General Andrew Jackson. *Poem of the South* was one of the first American works to include a Native American protagonist.[19]

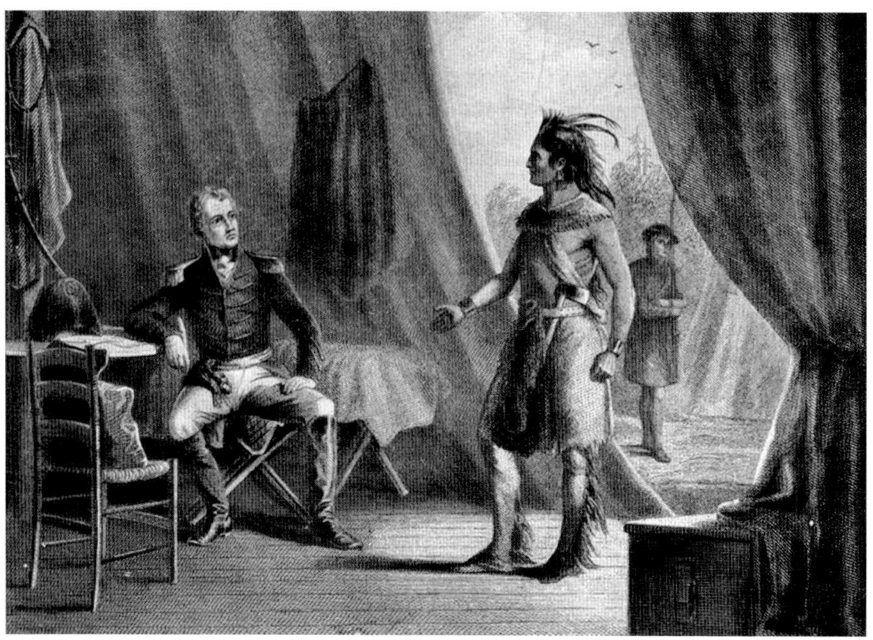

Weatherford surrenders to Andrew Jackson at Fort Jackson following the Battle of Horseshoe Bend. Jackson spares Weatherford from being killed by one of his soldiers. *Horseshoe Bend National Military Park.*

Menawa was a member of a high-ranking family, well respected by the Creeks and Americans. Menawa was famous for his prowess as a warrior along the Tennessee and Georgia frontiers. In his youth, he was known as Hothelya and Crazy Horse, nicknames from his raids into Tennessee, where he stole cattle and horses and brought them back into what is now Central Alabama. Although seriously wounded, he survived the Battle of Horseshoe Bend and subsequently served in the First Seminole War as an ally of the United States. He is believed to have died after Creek removal to the western territories in about 1843.

Fort Toulouse

Fort Toulouse was constructed by the French in 1717, located in the present Elmore County, near the town of Wetumpka. The French occupied the fort until the end of the French and Indian War. They used the structure as a stronghold in their attempt to gain control of the southeastern United States from the Spanish and English. In 1763, when the Treaty of Paris was signed,

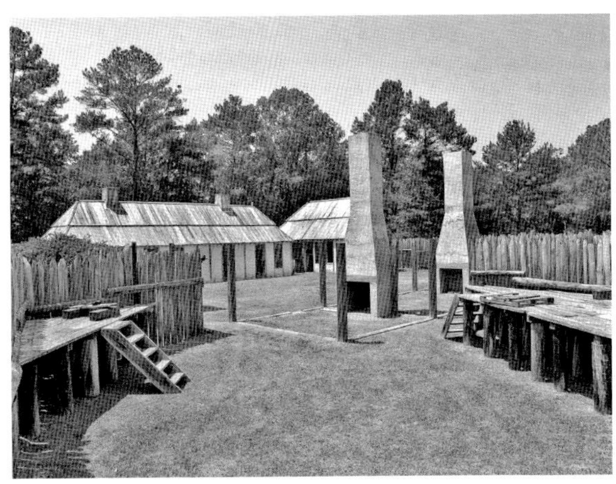

In 1814, after defeating the Creeks at the Battle of Horseshoe Bend, Andrew Jackson and his militia constructed Fort Jackson on the site of Fort Toulouse. *Donnie Shackleford, Encyclopedia of Alabama.*

the fort and surrounding land was transferred to the United States. Andrew Jackson and the Tennessee Militia constructed Fort Jackson on the site. After Jackson's victory over the Creek Nation in 1814, the Treaty of Fort Jackson was signed at the fort by the Creek leader Menawa and Andrew Jackson. After the treaty was signed, about one hundred militiamen decided their enlistment term was over. They left the fort and marched back to Tennessee. Their action weakened the defense of the garrison and infuriated Jackson. He captured, tried and executed six of them. His political opponents used this violent act against him when he ran for the presidency. However, his success as a military leader endeared him to the American people, and he became president in 1828. He proposed and passed the Indian Removal Act, which gave him the legal standing to remove the last of the Indians to the West in 1836.[20]

The Legend of Red Eagle

William Weatherford (1780–1824) was the son of a Scottish trader and a Creek woman. Weatherford was one of the Red Sticks who participated in the Fort Mims Massacre and leader of the Red Sticks at the Holy Ground Battle. The Fort Mims Massacre, on August 30, 1813, was the first major battle of the Creek War of 1813–14. William Weatherford (Red Eagle) led a force of about 700 Creek Indians in an attack and destruction of Fort Mims. The Red Sticks killed 250 settlers and their Indian allies, taking 100 captives. He became famous for his escape from American forces who chased him in retaliation for Fort Mims. "Weatherford escaped by leaping on horseback from a bluff into the Alabama River amid a hail of gunfire."

The name *Red Eagle* was based on his actions at the Battle of Econochaca, Holy Ground. The Third U.S. Infantry, Mississippi Militia and Cherokees chased him in retaliation for his part in the Fort Mims Massacre. To escape them, Weatherford leapt on a horse's back in a hail of fire and jumped over the bluff into the Alabama River. When he reemerged, he sat proudly on the back of the horse. The nickname "Red Eagle" appeared in A.B. Meek's poem honoring Red Eagle's adventures in the Indian wars and immortalizing his adventurous and courageous life.[21]

Tecumseh (1768–1813) was born in Ohio in 1768 but descended from Shawnee parents born at Souvanogee in present-day Tallapoosa County, Alabama. In 1787, Tecumseh visited Alabama and remained for two years, where he took part in the Cherokee and Creek festivities and fought with the tribes in "frontier" wars. Upon returning to Ohio, he fought there also in raids and battles, like the "attack on Fort Recovery" in 1794. When he returned to Alabama, he aligned himself with the Spaniards and British, who hated the emigrants. They traveled in large groups on the Federal Road, pushing the Indians off their land. Fueled by his hatred of the Americans and accompanied by a party of thirty warriors, he rode through Choctaw and Chickasaw country, trying to rally them to fight against the British. He fought in the War of 1812, allied with the British.[22]

Colonel Benjamin Hawkins, Indian agent over the southeastern territory, held his grand council at Tookabatchee. The gathering at the ancient capital consisted of five thousand Indian men in addition to whites and Blacks. By the time he reached Hickory Ground, Hawkins had gathered a large following. After Hawkins completed his address, Tecumseh marched into the square and spoke each day to the large gathering. After Hawkins finished his business and left to return to the "Agency," the grand council held a meeting in the great roundhouse. Tecumseh delivered fiery speeches, asking the Indians to join him in fighting against the Americans, who "had possessed the greater part of their country, turned its beautiful forests into large fields and stained their clear rivers with the washings of the soil."[23] He told them to leave behind the white man's customs and tools and dress in the animal clothing the Great Spirit had given them. The British would reward them "handsomely" for fighting against the Americans. Tecumseh's commanding appearance, majestic body and courageous words appealed to the large gathering of Indians, all except for Captain Isaacs, chief of Coosawda. In contempt of Tecumseh, he shook the giant buffalo horns he wore on his head. The meeting was not closed until Tenskwatawa, Tecumseh's younger brother and a Shawnee prophet, spoke.

The prophet told a story about how the Great Spirit sent Tecumseh to lead the Indians in their fight against the Americans. Speaking with furor, he said the Great Spirit said those who fought with him (Tecumseh) would be invincible. Tecumseh would stretch his arms toward heaven as a signal the war would begin. The Big Warrior at Tookabatcha was not convinced. Attempting further to persuade him to join the Red Sticks, Tecumseh said, "When I get there (Detroit), I will stamp my foot upon the ground, and shake down every house in Tookabatcha."[24] Miraculously, this prophecy did seem to be fulfilled by an earthquake at the predicted time. When Tecumseh would have arrived at Detroit and stamped his foot, an earthquake shook the ground at Tohopeka, and the houses fell. Believing what the prophet said, the Red Stick warriors were convinced they could fight against Jackson; they would be shielded from danger and safe from injury. Tecumseh fought at the Battle of Horseshoe Bend, but it was Menawa who led the Red Stick warriors.

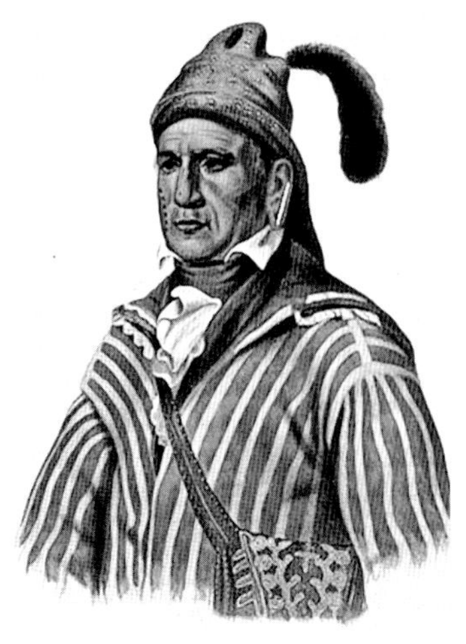

Menawa was forced to walk with other Creeks on the Trail of Tears. *Lithograph from painting by Charles Bird King, 1815–1826, Library of Congress.*

After the war, Menawa was given permission by the federal government to remain on the land that once belonged to the Creeks. But due to some confusion in the orders, he was ordered to join the rest of the Creeks on the Trail of Tears to a new homeland in the West. Menawa's last day on the Tallapoosa was described by Thomas L.M. Kenney:

> *Before he took final leave of the land of his fathers, he requested permission to revisit the Oakfuskee town, which had been his favorite residence. He remained there one night. The next morning he commenced the long-dreaded journey towards the place of exile. After crossing the Tallapoosa he seemed for some time abstracted and uneasy. His conduct was that of one who had forgotten something, and under this supposition it was proposed to him to return for the purpose of correcting the omission. But he said, "No! Last evening I saw the sun set for the last time, and its light shine upon the tree tops, and the land, and the water, that I am never to look upon again. No other evening will come, bringing to Menawa's eyes the rays of the settling sun upon the home he has left forever!"*[25]

Frontier Heroes at Tohopeka

Andrew Jackson's "reputation as a war hero began at the Battle of Horseshoe Bend and continued to grow. With the successful completion of the Creek War, Jackson was promoted to Major General in the United States Army for the duration of the War of 1812."[26] His military conquests catapulted him into the presidency of the United States of America in 1828. With the passage of his Indian Removal Act in 1830, Jackson began to evacuate the Native Americans from their homeland and allow white settlers to claim homesteads. The second Creek War began in 1836, when settlers were arriving in the area and attempting to force the Creeks off the land. They cheated and swindled Indians out of their money and land, inciting new skirmishes. Andrew Jackson used the circumstances to forcefully remove the Indians from their homes and send them west to join others who had left years earlier.

Major Lemuel Montgomery of the Thirty-Ninth was the first to mount the barricade, only to be shot dead. He was followed by **Ensign Sam Houston**, who, despite taking a barbed arrow to his thigh, dropped into the fort and cut down several Creeks with his saber. As other soldiers poured over the barricade, the young ensign reluctantly retired to seek a surgeon. Jackson rode up as Houston was being treated. Inquiring into the ensign's condition, Jackson ordered Houston not to return to the fray. The exchange marked the beginning of a warm friendship that would forever alter the destiny of the American West.

An impressive height—six feet, six inches in his stockings—Sam Houston led his platoon over the ramparts and fell on the inside. An Indian shot him in the leg with an arrow. After the Battle of Horseshoe Bend, Houston was elected the first president of the Republic of Texas and later elected senator from the state of Texas. Although Davy Crockett did not fight with Sam Houston at Horseshoe Bend, they both fought and died at the Alamo (February 23–March 6, 1836).

Dudleyville and the Floating Corpse

Twenty-eight-year-old Major Lemuel Purnell Montgomery fell at the Battle of Horseshoe Bend in March 1814 when a rifle ball slammed into his skull, killing him. Jackson was so deeply hurt by Montgomery's death that he wept over his body and referred to him as the "flower of his army." Montgomery was buried at the battle site. Twelve years later, he was disinterred and reburied at Dudleyville. Oddly, even though he was given a full military service, no marker was placed at the site. With no marker on the grave, the location was eventually forgotten. In the spring of 1886, an unusual amount of rain revealed a slight sink in the ground. A neighbor, Mr. Hall McIntosh; a physician, Dr. W.G. Carleton; and Reverend Jack Carleton discussed digging Montgomery up, placing him in a secure box and reburying him. They began digging in the vicinity where they believed him to be buried and came across the long bones of the arms and legs. They discovered fragments of the skull and spinal column. The metal buttons with the military insignia they found confirmed the bones belonged to Montgomery. Securing his remains, the men buried him again. But Montgomery would not lay undisturbed forever. In 1933, the Daughters of the Confederacy, in a formal ceremony, honored Montgomery with a marble marker on the site. After Horseshoe Bend was declared a National Military Park, about 1965, park service agents disinterred Montgomery's remains at Dudleyville and took them back to the park and buried him in the exact place where he was killed leading his men over the breastworks in 1814. After being moved three times over a period of 151 years, perhaps the poor man, or what is left of him, can rest in peace!

Preparing for Burial

Dudleyville is located twelve miles east/northeast of Dadeville, the county seat of Tallapoosa County. In the late 1700s and early 1800s, Dudleyville had an inn for travelers on the stagecoach line from West Point, Georgia, to Wetumpka and Montgomery, Alabama. Businesses included a buggy and wagon factory, a blacksmith shop and a tan yard. James Moore was the first known white settler in the Dudleyville area. Originally from Pennsylvania, he moved to Dudleyville in the 1790s. He took an Indian maiden for his wife and served as an Indian agent. Peter Dudleyville and Abraham Mordecai came to the town about the same time. Because Dudley was the first to operate a trading post in the area, the town was named *Dudleyville*.

Abraham Mordecai settled first at Coosada Bluff with his Indian wife and established a trading post, bartering for furs, hides and nut oils and then sending them to Mobile, Pensacola and Augusta by packhorse. Mordecai became infatuated with a beautiful young Indian squaw. When her husband learned Mordecai was having an affair with his wife, he dragged Mordecai out and beat him brutally. He cut off his ear and, with the assistance of other

Indian men, threw his body over a high bluff and left him to die. Mordecai managed to survive the beating and regain his health with the care of his faithful Indian wife. He was described by all who knew him as "eccentric." He built his casket several years before his death and used it as a dining table. He delighted in demonstrating to his guests how well his body fit into the casket. He lived to be ninety-seven or ninety-eight and eventually was buried in the casket. His grave is in the old Dudleyville Cemetery.

Chapter 2

WHERE ALABAMA BEGAN

In the late 1700s, the frontier town called Hobuckintoopa was located on a limestone bluff overlooking the Tombigbee River. The Choctaw Trading House was the first building in Hobuckintoopa. The high bluffs attracted the ships and smaller vessels of the French, British, Spanish and Americans; each country, in turn, ruled Hobuckintoopa Bluff. In 1772, the British sent Bernard Romans, an English surveyor, to assess the value of Hobuckintoopa. Romans observed, "Sloops and schooners may come up to this rapid: therefore, I judge some considerable settlement will take place."[27] Roman's words rang true as ships made their way to the bluff. Deep-bottom ships could go no farther than the rapid due to shallow rocks and shoals. Supplies then were transferred by shallow vessels farther upriver.

Hobuckintoopa was part of the larger area of French land in the Tombigbee area. The French built a fort on the Tombigbee River in Sumter County, believing the location offered protection from the British traders and unfriendly Indians. In 1789, the Spanish gained control of the site and built a fortification that they named Fort Estefan in honor of Mobile's governor, Esteban Rodriguez Miro. Earthen works were built for protection, a church for worship and a home for the fort's commandant, Antonio Palaas. Fort Esteban under Spanish rule remained in place for a decade. Following a land dispute, a survey was done, and ownership transferred to America.

On May 5, 1799, at this remote site, a formal, military ceremony took place. American lieutenant John McClary waited as Palaas "struck the Spanish colors for the last time and led his troops out.…McClary then paraded his men in and raised the flag of the United States over the site for the first time."[28] The land became American property and was renamed St. Stephens, marking where Alabama began.

Alabama Fever

In 1817, Mississippi Territory was recognized as a state by the United States government, and a portion of the land was carved out to create Alabama Territory. With the largest population in the old Mississippi Territory, St. Stephens was chosen to serve as Alabama's territorial capital, and William Wyatt Bibbs was appointed governor. Exchanges between Indians and settlers continued at the old trading post, which additionally served as an Indian agency. George Strother Gaines was put in charge of the government's business. Settlers competed furiously for acres of land to purchase and cultivate their cotton crops. They created what may have been the first land boom in the country. The term *Alabama Fever* was coined to describe the large influx of settlers into Alabama territory.[29]

St. Stephens: "A Thriving Metropolis"

St. Stephens grew rapidly. Within a year, the town had a population of "several thousand residents" and at least five hundred homes. There were medical offices, law offices, Tombeck's bank, two hotels, twenty stores and a theater that performed popular plays such as *She Stoops to Conquer*.[30] The local Thespian Society of St. Stephens performed comedies like *The Day After the Wedding* or *A Wife's First Lesson*. Tickets were one dollar each. St. Stephens could boast of four different newspapers; the last was the *Halcyon and Tombeckbe Advertiser*, by the publisher Thomas Eastin. The town expanded quickly with new enterprises, such as J.H. Dearing and Company, which, in May 1820, launched one of the first steamboats on the Tombigbee River. The town was home to several notorieties, such as "Henry Hitchcock, the first attorney general of Alabama and later chief justice of the state Supreme Court."[31] Other "firsts" include the building of Alabama's first steamboat. The *Alabama* was built in St. Stephens in February 1818 and launched on the Alabama River with an excited gathering of citizens looking on.

The steamboat was a cheap and efficient means of transporting cotton to the Mobile port. Ideal landings like St. Stephens were situated on high bluffs rising from the river. The steamboats loaded cotton from the nearly three hundred landings along the Tombigbee River and the nearly two hundred landings along the Alabama River before navigating downstream to Mobile. In addition to loading cotton, the steamboats restocked the supply of firewood needed to keep the boilers operating and dispensing steam. Steamboats also sent cargos of domestic and farm supplies back upstream.[32] Steamboats increased farmers' ability to ship their cotton crops to the Mobile port and, as a result, gained more profit for their product. Steamboats held the lead in shipping goods until the train and railroad tracks provided a quicker and more comfortable means of travel. Travel by steamboats seemed to be safe until the explosion of the *Sultana* near Cahaba as Union prisoners were being taken home. St. Stephens residents enjoyed the hustle and bustle of the thriving metropolis that attracted visitors to the state capital. They often stayed at the Douglas's hotel, shopped at the local stores and attended a play at the Halcyon theater.

The Curse of Lorenza Dow

The small town possessed natural beauty and a magnificent view of the Tombigbee River from the bluff but, in the view of some visitors, had little refinement. In 1804, Ephraim Kirby, the first superior judge of Mississippi Territory, described St. Stephens's inhabitants in a letter to President Thomas Jefferson as "illiterate, wild, and savage, of depraved morals, unworthy of public confidence or private esteems, litigious, disunited, and knowing each other, universally distrustful of each other."[33] On December 25, 1804, Lorenza Dow arrived, bringing with him his Bible and his journal, in which he wrote a favorable first impression of St. Stephens, the bluff and the Tombigbee River: "it will be a place of fame in time." Dow set about preaching with all the zeal of a frontier preacher who regarded the citizenry of the entire town as potential members of his flock. For all his pomp and polished rhetoric, the people thought he was odd in his manner, suggesting he thought he was better than they were. He condemned their actions as "wicked" and preached fervently about the evils of "frequenting local taverns on the sabbath rather than attending church." As he persisted with his rantings, the men took it upon themselves to teach him a lesson. They tarred and feathered Lorenza, put him on a raft and sent him down the Tombigbee River. Dow cursed St. Stephens, warning that the "bats and owls will inhabit the city and make it their home and pestilence will soon drive the inhabitants from the city." Later, when the capital was moved from St. Stephens to Cahaba and residents faced many challenges, they may have thought of Dow's curse and wished they had treated him more kindly.

> The History of Methodism *described Lorenza Dow's appearance as follows: He wore his hair parted in the middle, and wore it hanging down on his neck and shoulders. His face was radiant with expressions of human kindness. He was a rough man, he was an honest, truthful, candid man with generous impulses and kindly feelings. He had in him the impulses imparted to him by an endowment of Christian grace. He was a man of Christian experience. He was a Christian. He was Lorenza Dow.*[34]

Dow was the first preacher in the wilderness of Mississippi and Alabama and presumed to be the first preacher in the Tombigbee area. He produced excitement and converted many people to Christian beliefs. He loved the Methodist Church and often refused any compensation for his preaching. He even sold part of his belongings to help a community build a new church.

St. Stephens has no ghost stories, tales of apparitions or orbs that astonished visitors. No strange occurrences were reported other than the odd preacher Lorenza Dow and the curse he placed on St. Stephens, but the town has its mysteries, like the Indian Baths. Some people credit the Choctaw with carving the rectangular basins filled with mineral water. Visitors can still see the Indian Baths today. The searches continue to identify part of the town's past in pieces of broken pottery, tools and jewelry. In a recent excavation, archaeologists discovered European tools, causing them to believe the Spanish dug the tubs rather than the Indians. The origins of the Indian baths may be a mystery to leave with St. Stephens as the Choctaw left their ancestral lands when they headed west in the 1830s. Surely, the French, British, Spanish and English took stories with them of the time they lived in the wilderness that later became the territorial capital where Alabama began.[35]

The St. Stephens Historical Park, sponsored by the Alabama Historical Association, is open to visitors who wish to explore the remains of the old town. Surprisingly, there are a few structures left to see: the Indian Baths, remains of cellars, the original town well and old headstones with names that are legible. Markers indicate where town buildings once stood. To encourage visitors, the park has family outings and special events for entertainment.

The archaeological excavations occasionally yield a relic, but none suggest a ghost ever resided in St. Stephens. Even the ghosts, if they ever existed, seem to have abandoned St. Stephens. Perhaps they too were restless in that remote place and followed the town residents to the new Stephens. Others might say it is more likely they traveled to old Cahaba, Alabama's most haunted town, and joined the ghosts there.

A Shift in Politics

St. Stephens's prominence as the state capital was short-lived due to a shift in politics. Alabama governor William Bibb gained a great deal of political power when he served as the first territorial governor of Alabama. His influence increased when he became governor of the state of Alabama. His promotion of Cahaba as the site for Alabama's state capital carried considerable political weight. Conversely, St. Stephens's supporters advocated that the capital remain in the same place. The proponents for moving the capital stated the risk of contracting yellow fever (malaria) was greater in St. Stevens than in Cahaba because of frequent flooding. They stressed the inconvenience for legislators to get to the capital buildings and conduct business. The opposing representatives joked that the legislators had to travel by boat and enter the capital building through a second-floor window. St. Stephens's residents opposed the statements and insisted newspapers exaggerated the situation. When all the reasons were stated, the legislators chose Cahaba as the site for Alabama's capital. Not entirely defeated, the dissenting legislators wrote a clause into the agreement that

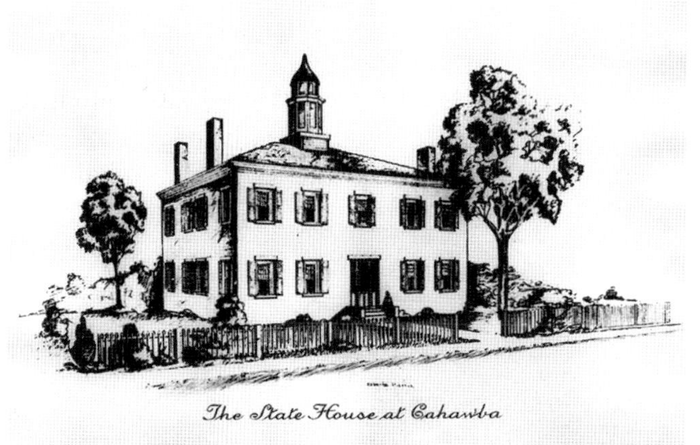

The State House. Alabama's first capitol had a small copper dome on top, which now sits atop the Christian Methodist Episcopal Church in Lowndesboro. *Alabama Department of Archives and History, Al.com/Living/2016/08/17.*

reconsideration of the capital's location should be made at the end of the first term.

In 1819, when Alabama became a state, the first state constitutional convention was held in the temporary capital of Huntsville, Alabama. Two lobbying groups, the Alabama Cahaba river basin group and the Warrior-Tombigbee group, debated where the permanent capital would be located. A board of commissioners was assigned the task of finding the "most eligible *scite* [*sic*] for seat of territorial government." Governor Bibb used every tool he had to win over any objections to Cahaba as the site. He won the contest with the large grant of land President James Monroe gave to him. Bibb proposed dividing land into lots and selling them to bring in enough money to finance construction of the capitol. When Monroe more than doubled the federal land grant, the matter was settled. Cahaba became Alabama's first state capital.[36]

St. Stephens was settled in a distant past where, at one time, Indians and settlers met at the Choctaw Trading Post to trade furs, weapons and clothing. At the time, traders and visitors could not go beyond the shoals in their shallow bottom boats safely, but when ships were developed that could go over rocks into upper streams, St. Stephen lost its monopoly on the river trade. Traders could now pass by Hobuckintoopa and take their "wares" up the river to trade for furs. Due to its prominence on the Choctaw Bluff initially, St. Stephens served well as the territorial capital.

OLD CAHABA: ALABAMA'S MOST HAUNTED TOWN

> *Until you walk where your ancestors walked, you can never truly understand the written record….Many of the best stories from the past, and many of the solutions to history's most intriguing mysteries are not found in any book or archive; instead, they lie buried beneath the soil, waiting for archaeology to carefully uncover them.*[37]

Cahaba's settlers and plantation owners were not the first people to live on this historic site. Alabama's first governor, William Wyatt Bibb, and the men who worked with him in laying out the town unearthed the remains of a large Indian village. Archaeologists date the ghost town back to the Mississippian Period (AD 100–1550), the mound building era. The Alabama

Archeological Commission reported that excavations uncovered evidence that "as early as 4,000 years ago, Prehistoric Indians occupied Cahawba." They found a moat, palisade and ceremonial mound.

The ancient Indian town on which Cahaba was built suffered the first of several mysterious occurrences that made Cahaba famous as Alabama's most haunted town. Many archaeologists and historians believe this may have been the site of Mabila, where thousands of Indians were killed by Hernando de Soto and his conquistadors in 1450. De Soto's chroniclers recorded the story of Mabila and what may have been the bloodiest battle in Alabama history. Cahaba was built on a large mound covering the ancient Indian town, but no conclusive evidence has proved the town was Mabila. Alabama's first state capital, Cahaba (also spelled Cahawba), comes from the Choctaw language, meaning "water above." Located at the juncture of Alabama and Cahaba Rivers, the town became prosperous during the time it served as the state's first capital (1819–25) but withered when the state politicians, businesses and many residents moved to Tuscaloosa. However, Cahaba became prosperous again in the 1840s and 1850s, when large farms in Alabama grew hundreds of acres of cotton to be picked, bundled and transported via steamboat to Mobile and sold for high profits.

The mansions in Cahaba were some of the largest and finest in the state. Ferries and steamboats operated on both Cahaba and Alabama Rivers nearby. Built in 1849, the Old Cahaba Methodist Episcopal Church served residents of Alabama's first capital. Streets bore the names of trees: pine, oak, chestnut and mulberry. Although time altered the landscape and destroyed most of the fine old homes, the landscape of Old Cahaba remains beautiful, with Spanish moss hanging from branches of huge old trees and flowers blooming near old house sites.[38]

Today, the Alabama Historical Commission owns and operates this significant archaeological site. Archaeologists recently discovered Cahaba was built upon the remains of an earlier ghost town. Some experts believe the earlier village was "Mabila," the famous Native American village destroyed by Spanish explorer Hernando de Soto in 1540. More surprising is the discovery that Gov. William Wyatt Bibb (1819–1820) and his surveyors not only found the remains of this ancient village, but they incorporated the old earthworks into the centerpiece of Cahaba's town plan. Apparently, Bibb hoped to build Alabama's statehouse atop the ancient Indian mound. He planned to use a semicircular moat dug around the ancient village three centuries earlier to restrict the grounds of the statehouse.[39]

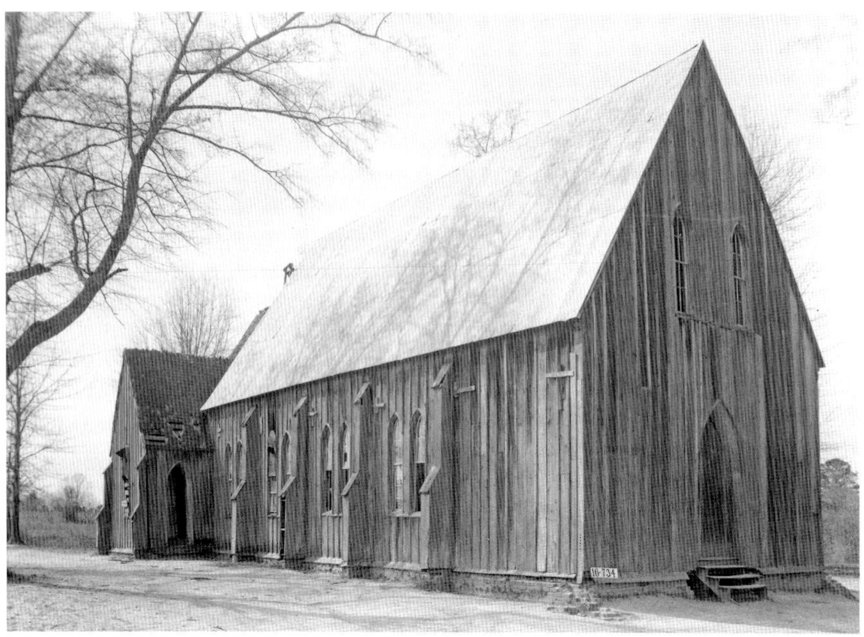

Old Cahaba's Methodist Episcopal Church was built in 1849, served Old Cahaba for twenty years and was destroyed by fire in 1954. *Alabama Department of Archives and History, Al.com/Living/2016/08/17.*

Governor William Wyatt Bibb was appointed Alabama's territorial governor and then Alabama's first state governor. Through his political connections with the Broad River Group and the Alabama-Cahaba group, Bibb obtained a federal land grant from President Monroe for the site of the capital to be at the confluence of the Alabama and Cahaba Rivers. The opposing group advocated for the capital to be placed at Huntsville, stating the ground was higher and would be safe from flooding. With a significant increase in the grant to his advantage, Bibb suggested that the town lots be sold and the money used to build the town. The opposing side (Tombigbee) relinquished its choice and agreed Cahaba should be the site for Alabama's first state capital. However, they approved only $10,000 for building the capital building since they viewed it as temporary. The agreement included a clause that permitted legislators to change the location if no one objected. Cahaba lost its chief supporter, Governor Bibb, in 1820 when he died after following from his horse. Tragically, Bibb did not survive to see Cahaba's prosperity as the state capital or later as a boomtown when settlers rushed in to claim farmland in Alabama's Black Belt counties.

Initially, the federal land office in Cahaba sold lots for $1.25 an acre, a price that quickly rose to $70.00 an acre. Unimproved lots brought $5,000.00 or more by 1822. Bibb modeled Cahaba after Philadelphia, with streets and avenues lined with trees. Lovely homes were built along the streets as the town developed stores, "two newspapers, a theater, state bank, hotels, two ferries, doctor offices, a ladies' academy, and an imposing two-story brick capital."[40]

In 1825, Cahaba welcomed the Marquis de Lafayette and his son, who were visiting cities in the United States on a "triumphal tour." The state of Alabama spared no expense in honoring the distinguished hero of the French and American Revolutions. The state spent $17,000 on the tour, while having spent only $10,000 on constructing the state capitol buildings and town of Cahaba. Arriving aboard the steamship *Anderson*, Lafayette and his son were welcomed with bells ringing and cannons booming, with cheers from the crowd. Residents enjoyed a public barbecue with their famous guests. In the evening, Cahaba's most affluent citizens attended an "elaborate" dinner and ball.[41]

Lafayette: Alabama's First Marathon Dancer

Kathryn Tucker Windham, author of *13 Alabama Ghosts and Jeffrey*, observed, "Families all over Alabama have great-great grandmothers (or is it three greats, now?) who danced with Lafayette." They claimed to have an invitation or letter confirming she danced with Lafayette. The truth is, if Lafayette had danced with the ancestors who claimed that honor, he would have been the state's first marathon dancer.[42]

In her book *Alabama: One Big Front Porch*, Windham shared another humous story about Lafayette's welcome celebration. Amid the crowd gathered on Goat Hill, Captain Thomas Carr, a Revolutionary War veteran himself, attempted unsuccessfully to push through the crowd. Seeing a nearby well, he climbed up onto the curbing to see what was going on. He was so intent on observing Lafayette that he lost his balance and fell into the well. Governor Pickens stopped his welcome speech and helped "fish" Carr out of the well. He was unharmed but quickly became famous for making a "big splash" at the event.[43]

Cahaba had several artesian wells. The most famous was the Perine well, named for the owner, E.M. Perine, a wealthy merchant. Perine's well measured seven hundred to nine hundred feet deep and was believed to be the deepest known artesian well in the world at the time. Perine piped water from the well throughout his home. Due to his remarkable ingenuity, he and his family lived in "the first air-conditioned dwelling in Alabama."[44]

Fresh water from the artesian wells was a blessing. Water in Cahaba was also a curse with the constant fear of flooding and the danger of yellow fever. In 1822, water from the Alabama and Cahaba Rivers flooded into town, separating the business section from the residential. Although the flooding was not severe, the event gave support for people who wanted to move the capital to another location.

As Cahaba progressed in expanding businesses, entertainment and merchandizing, cotton was a booming business, and farmers needed a warehouse to store the cotton before it could be transported to Mobile. The construction of a warehouse was interrupted by the Civil War. Eventually, the warehouse was finished, but it was never used for cotton. Instead, in June 1863, the building became known as the Cahaba Federal Prison.[45] Cahaba farmers began building a railroad to transport their cotton. This project, too, was interrupted by the Confederacy. The railroad spikes, bolts, nuts and rails were appropriated by the Confederate Congress to use in building a railroad line connecting Selma and Demopolis.

Castle Morgan

The local people changed the name "Cahaba Prison" to "Castle Morgan," possibly named for Confederate general John Hunt Morgan, who escaped from the Ohio State Penitentiary. The fifteen-thousand-square-foot building was anything but a castle. Camp surgeon R.H. Whitfield reported the filthy condition in which 660 Union soldiers were held prisoner. Dirty water ran into the building from the street. With only one fireplace, there was inadequate heat; they had little food and medical care. With bedding or straw for only 432 bunk spaces, hundreds were left to sleep on the filthy, damp floor. Despite the horrific conditions at Castle Morgan, records show only between 142 and 147 men died there. But the worst lay ahead when, on April 27, 1865, 2,300 prisoners from Castle Morgan and Andersonville were being transported home on the steamboat *Sultana*.[46] The men and one thousand bushels of fuel overloaded the 260-foot steamboat as they began the trip to Cairo, Illinois, where they would be released. When a photographer

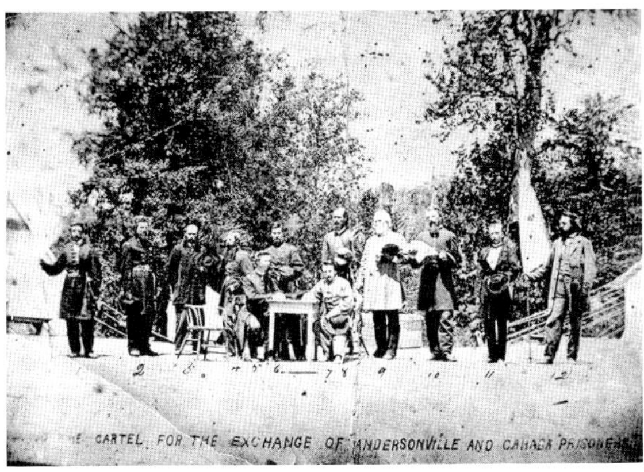

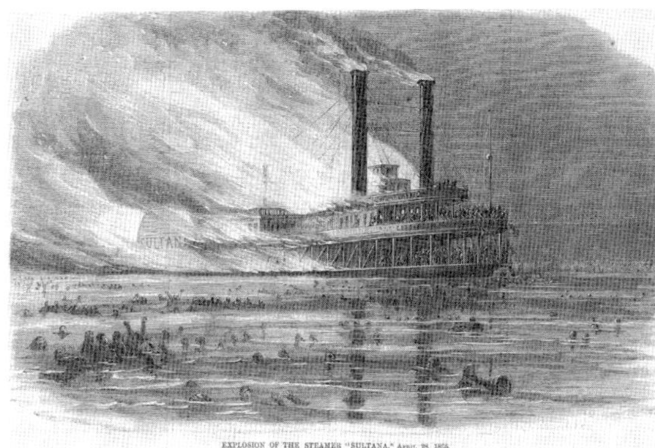

Top: A historical marker shows where the Andersonville and Fort Morgan Civil War officers and soldiers met and exchanged prisoners in 1865. *Legendsofamerica.com/Andersonville-georgia/2.*

Bottom: The explosion of the steamer *Sultana*, April 28, 1865, the largest steamboat disaster in Alabama, killed 1,600; 520 survived and were hospitalized. *Encyclopedia of Alabama.*

was setting up his camera, hundreds of men rushed to one side to be in the picture. The boat barely missed capsizing.[47]

Eight miles past Memphis, the three boilers exploded in rapid succession. The buildup of mud and sediment from the river in the fire-tube boilers created enough pressure in the overheated flue to blow out sediment, and a massive burst of steam caused the explosions. There were only 520 survivors, out of whom 200 died in the hospital. Others drowned. On April 27, 600 passengers went down with the *Sultana*, one of the most horrific accidents in the history of steamboats.[48]

Why Cahaba Is Haunted

The ghosts of the Federal prisoners who died in Castle Morgan may have returned to Cahaba seeking revenge for the injustices they suffered. The ghosts of the 1,600 Federal prisoners who died in the explosion of the steamboat

Sultana returned to caution others not to travel by steamboat. Ghosts of the Indians who once lived in the large Indian town now buried under Cahaba may have been offended by what they viewed as the desecration of their ancestors' land when Governor Bibb and his crew began digging in the soil and likely their burial place. The ghost tales originating at Cahaba captured the interest of Kathryn Tucker Windham. She included two of the best-known in her book *13 Alabama Ghosts and Jeffrey*: "The Specter in the Maze at Cahaba" and "The Return of the Ruined Banker."

How the President of the First National Bank of Selma Wound Up in Castle Morgan Prison

Sturdivant Hall in Selma was the setting for the following ghost story in Kathryn Tucker Windham's *13 Alabama Ghosts and Jeffrey*. In its day, the hall was one of the most elegant homes in the Black Belt. John Parkman, president of the First National Bank of Selma, lived in Sturdivant Hall with his wife and two daughters, Emily Norris Parkman and Maria Hunter Parkman. The bank had a capital of $100,000. Cotton was yielding such high profits at the time that John decided to invest a large part of the bank's assets in cotton. When the price of cotton dropped from thirty or thirty-five to fifteen or eighteen cents per pound, John did not have the money to cover the loss. Learning of the deficit, General Wager Swayne, commanding officer, closed the bank and arrested John Parkman. General Swayne and his men took Parkman to Cahaba and imprisoned him at Castle Morgan, the Confederate prison for Yankee prisoners.

When tours are made at Sturdivant, some guests say they feel cold air rush past them. The guide tells the story of John Parkman and how he escaped from Castle Morgan only to be shot and killed. The new owner of Sturdivant Hall retained Parkman's servants, who reported seeing Parkman walking restlessly about the grounds. At other times, they saw him gazing from the cupola on top of the house. Some people believe he did not like strangers in his home; others think that he was looking for someone to clear his name and restore him to his respected status as a bank president and resident of his beloved Sturdivant Hall.[49]

"The Specter of the Maze" in Windham's *13 Alabama Ghosts and Jeffrey* is set in Cahaba. As the leader of the Cahaba Rifles, Fifth Alabama Regiment, Colonel Pegues was well respected for his military role in the Civil War. Pegues's house and grounds were favorite places for social events. The

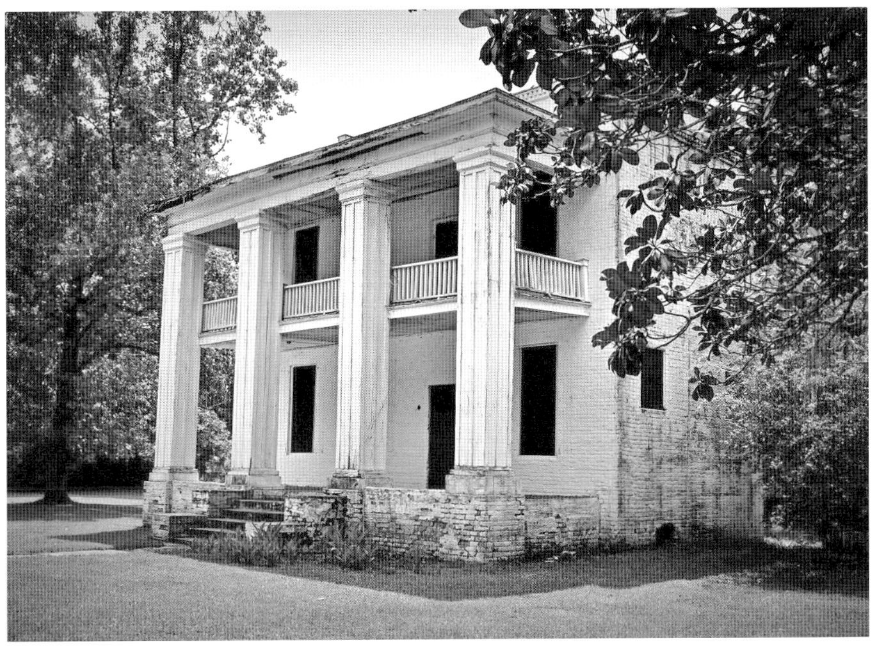

The Barker slave quarters at Kirkpatrick mansion were built in 1860 and burned during the 1930s. *cahawba.com.historyandlegacy*.

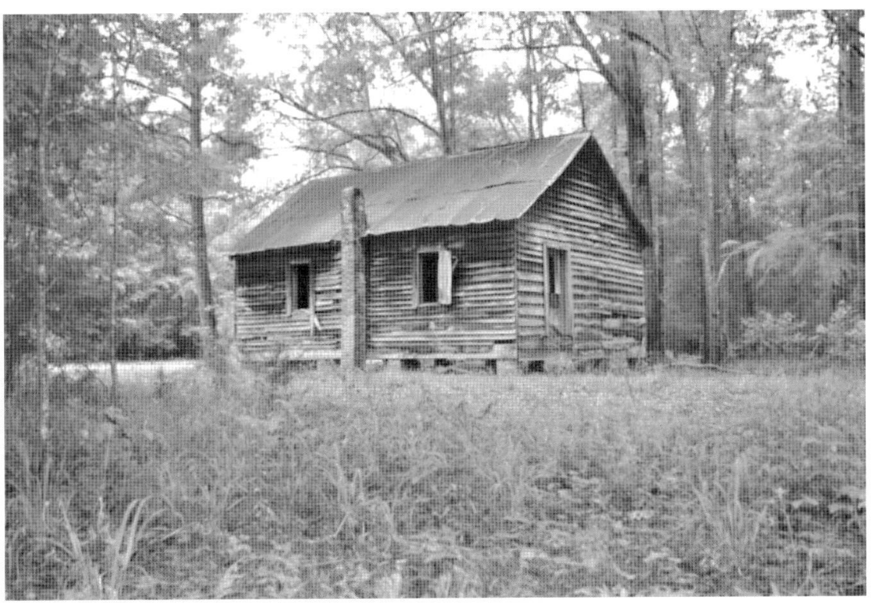

Today, the school that Black citizens built for their children is one of only three structures still standing at the Old Cahaba site. *cahawba.com.historyandlegacy*.

many varieties of trees—cedars, pines, magnolias—with rows of hedges were magnificent. The decorative fountains and scented vines and flowers created a beautiful, fragrant scene. Walking through the rows of hedges provided private time for visitors. In 1862, a young couple reported seeing an orb darting toward them and then receding into the background. People speculated that the orb was the apparition of Colonel Pegues. The date fit the time of Pegues being wounded at the Battle of Gaines' Mill in Virginia that year; he reportedly died two weeks later. Why Pegues returned could have been from a love of his beautiful estate or to welcome the many guests who enjoyed visiting his home. Another reason may have been to warn recruits of the dangers of war.[50]

Cahaba's grand days were over when the county seat was moved to Selma in 1866. White businessmen, newspaper editors and officeholding men moved too. The newly emancipated slaves used skills they had learned to rebuild dilapidated buildings, such as the courthouse. In the group of skilled African workers were bricklayers, carpenters and blacksmiths. What

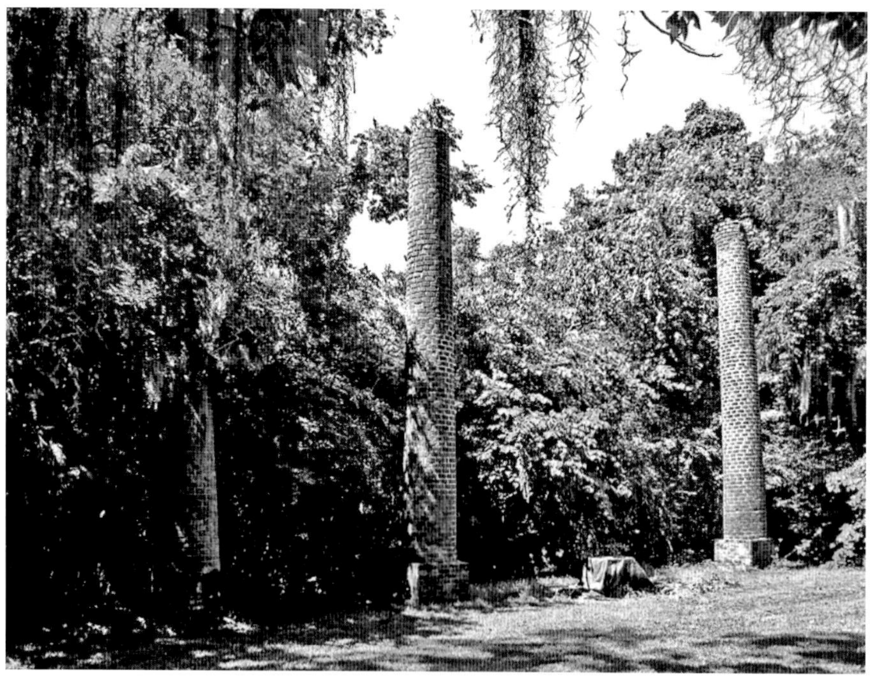

Brick pillars are all that remain of the Cahaba home of the Crocheron family, which may have survived because the custom-shaped bricks could not be used to build other structures. *al.com/living/2016/08/7_weird_things_youlllearning_at.html.*

was left of Cahaba was now in the hands of the freedmen group, who attempted to rebuild the town from the scraps of wood from dilapidated buildings. They built a school that remains in the park today. The Barker slave quarters, built in 1860 at the Kirkpatrick Mansion, were destroyed by fire in the 1930s. The small copper top of the first capitol building was moved from Cahaba to Lowndesboro and placed on top of the Christian Methodist Episcopal Church, where it sits today. It took approximately one month to move the top forty-five miles. The freedmen became landowners, lawyers and politicians, holding influential offices like "Jordan Hatcher, who was Cahaba's postmaster, before being appointed to the Constitutional Convention of lawyers and state legislators."[51]

What Remains

Cahaba is important because of its history as Alabama's first state capital and for the archaeological remains of the town and those of the old Indian town on which Cahaba was built. An antebellum river town, Cahaba at the peak of prosperity made Dallas the richest county in the state. The river produced the largest diversity of fish population of any river the same size. "Cahaba is the longest free-flowing river in Alabama and has received attention from environmentalists throughout the nation."[52] Cahaba is a popular archaeological excavation site. Through the studies of archaeologists, conservationists, historians and anthropologists, more important discoveries are sure to be made, with additional theories proved or disproved.[53]

Chapter 3

MINING

Gold veins were formed in quartz and ore at the same time as the great Appalachian Mountains. The tons of rock had some gold and other ores, like silica and copper. The picturesque mountains and rock cliffs stretched into the foothills of Alabama, where gold was discovered in the southern Piedmont decades before the 1849 California Gold Rush. The first gold strike in the southern Piedmont was on the Reed Farm in Cabarrus County, North Carolina, when in 1799, twelve-year-old Conrad Reed pulled a large, odd-shaped rock from the meadow where he was fishing. When the rock was identified as gold, neighbors began digging up their fields in hopes of "striking it rich." Struck with gold fever, thousands of people rushed into North Carolina. In Georgia, in 1828, while hunting, Benjamin Parks stumbled over an unusual stone near Licklog in the present Lumpkin County. The name "Licklog" was changed to Dahlonega, a Cherokee word meaning "yellow money." In 1832, gold was discovered at Villa Rica (Spanish for "City of Riches").

Alabama Gold Belt Counties

From 1828 to 1830, miners crossed from Georgia goldfields into Alabama eager to find new gold mining sites at the same time land was opening for settlers. Hordes of people rushed onto land that once belonged to the great

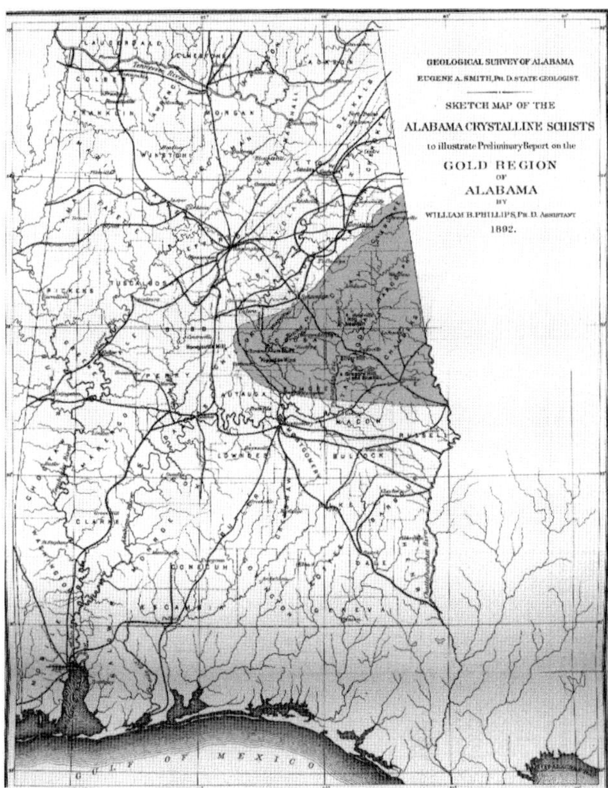

Alabama gold belt map of the nine counties where gold was located on what was Creek land until the defeat at Horseshoe Bend. *Alabama Department of Archives and History*.

Creek Nation but was ceded after their defeat at the Battle of Horseshoe Bend. The United States government and the Native Americans agreed on treaty terms, but the American government broke each, one by one. In 1830, President Andrew Jackson passed the Indian Removal Act to evacuate the Cherokees from their homeland in Georgia, the Muscogee from Alabama and other tribes. The law was passed in 1830 and enacted in 1836 to drive Native Americans from their ancestral lands to California on the walk that became known as the Trail of Tears due to brutal weather conditions, starvation and exhaustion.

Settlers seized acres of the open land and rushed to the federal land office in Montgomery to register legal claims on the land. They established homes and farming communities. When cotton prices were high, they were farmers. When cotton prices were low, they were miners. Two gold rushes occurred in Alabama: Arbacoochee in Cleburne County and Goldville in Tallapoosa County. The first authenticated discovery of gold in Alabama was made by the nephew and namesake of Governor William Bibb and his father-in-law, Todd Robinson. The discovery of gold was authenticated by the *Niles Herald*, which reported the event.

> *Wyatt and Robinson collected their first gold on a tributary of Chestnut Creek, part of an eighty-acre tract they had purchased in the fall of 1830 for $100; it was this sight* [sic] *that produced the "specimen of pure virgin gold" that Wyatt took to the Mobile Register's office in the spring of 1831....The U.S. mint in Philadelphia received its first shipment of gold from Alabama—thirty-one ounces of gold amalgam and dust which the mint assigned a coinage value of $559.*[54]

Despite the excitement of finding gold on their land in old Autauga County (now Chilton County), the two men had a short mining career. Like the miners who followed them, they worked for a brief time. Then, deciding that farming was a better investment of their time and money, they abandoned mining and found new fields to plow.

ARBACOOCHEE: ALABAMA'S FIRST GOLD RUSH TOWN

Miners who found their way to Cleburne County were more fortunate than Bibb and Robinson in their mining endeavor. Established in 1835, Arbacoochee was a small community located between the Georgia line and the Talladega Mountains in Cleburne County, named after the old Indian town Abihkuchi, meaning "a pile at the base." As people learned of the discovery of gold in Arbacoochee, they rushed to claim a piece of the land and begin digging. The camp grew into a large mining town, bustling with people and business, with a population of five thousand farmers and gold miners. They swarmed over the land, laying claim to what appeared to them to be a good mining site. They built temporary homes, sometimes pitching a tent at the entrance of their claim to stop any intruder. Arbacoochee had two churches and five saloons, a school, a fire department, two hotels, two mining equipment stores, a racetrack, twenty general mercantile stores and over one hundred permanent homes. Miners worked from dawn to dusk and continued into the night, digging by lantern, determined to find gold.[55]

The community of Arbacoochee in Cleburne County was a bustling town of nearly 5,000 people during the 1840s. The economies of these towns centered on the gold mines, with mining companies paying between $0.75 and $1.75 per day in wages during the peak of production in the mid-1840s. Some of the larger mining camps gave rise to various gambling establishments, saloons, and brothels.[56]

Citizens lived in small frame houses or in tents. When the gold rush began in California, Arbacoochee was quickly abandoned and never regained its former glory. There is only one building remaining at the present time and is in bad condition. It is a two-story brick building with a gabled tin roof. It was built as a general merchandise store, the proprietor lived on the second floor. The walls are 3 layers of brick thick. Although the structure has been burned out twice, the exterior has remained virtually unchanged since 1849. Many of the holes and tunnels used by the miners are still evident along the road. Deep in the woods near the building is the "Glory Hole," the largest crevice in the area. Gold mining continued in spurts until the early 20th century. Tourists still come occasionally hoping to strike it rich.

According to local citizens, the largest piece of gold found east of the Mississippi was found at Arbacoochee.[57]

Old mining sites in Cleburne County and Tallapoosa County are now located on privately owned property. Miners quickly abandoned a site that produced only a small amount of gold. They packed up their scant belongings and headed out to a new spot that looked more promising. A few miners who stayed at the same site were occasionally rewarded with a substantial discovery, like the Cleburne miner who cleaned over eleven pounds of gold in one day. That evening, he went to a local establishment to celebrate his good fortune. A free-for-all fight broke out, and he was killed before he had the opportunity to enjoy his riches. The tale ends on a sad note, as a heavy rain fell that night and washed away any means of recognizing the site. Was he killed because someone planned to seize his claim, or was he simply a casualty of involvement in a drunken barroom brawl? The irony was the discovery of gold and the following celebration resulting in his death—all in the same day!

GOLDVILLE: ALABAMA'S SECOND GOLD RUSH TOWN

Goldville is located northeast of Alexander City, near Highway 49, which crosses into Clay County. In the 1800s, gold miners crossed over the Ashland Plateau from Georgia and entered the gold mining district in Tallapoosa County that included Goldville, Hog Mountain, Ely Pits Birdsong, Log Pits and Dutch Bend mines. In 1842, gold was discovered near Goldville. Miners rushed in to stake a claim. By 1845, the population had reached 3,000 to 3,500. The town had at least fourteen stores, several saloons and gambling establishments, two hotels and a pit for cockfighting. State geologist Michael Tuomey described the most productive vein, Log Pit, as having a depth of 105 feet and a thickness from 2 to 4 feet. The pit was discovered by accident when a curious miner broke off a piece of what he thought to be a rotten log. Instead of wood, he found gold in the large quartz outcropping. Other pits in the Goldville district were Birdsong (named for its owner, Edward Birdsong), Mahan and Jones. The town of Goldville was incorporated twice, first on January 25, 1843. Then, decades after the gold mining activity was in the past, Goldville was incorporated the second time on July 9, 1973.[58]

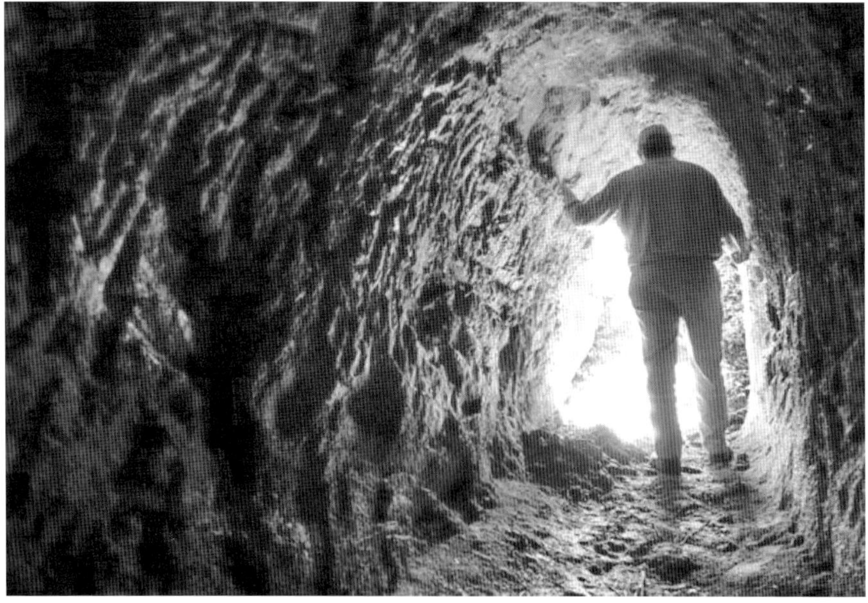

Gold light inside an old tunnel at Goldville, Tallapoosa County, the site of Alabama's second gold rush. *Encyclopedia of Alabama.*

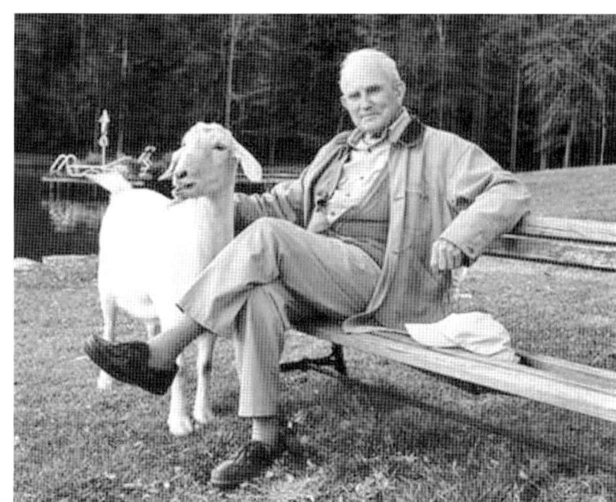

Former governor John Patterson on his Cragford farm at Goldville. The estimated town population in 2020 was fifty-four. *Picture donated to B.B. Comer Memorial Library by Patterson family.*

In the year 2000, the population was thirty-seven people; the 2010 census count was fifty-five, not counting the pet goat. Former governor John Patterson has a ranch house on the old Patterson Farm at Cragford just a few miles from Goldville. The land is pocked with holes where gold miners dug hoping to strike it rich back in the gold rush days. Standing in the crossroads at Goldville, looking in any of the four directions, one might find it impossible to envision thousands of people living there, frequenting the mining supply store, general merchandise stores or saloons, or picture people riding horses and buggies on dirt streets. The residents prospered well enough to support the town establishments. Drawn to a town named Goldville, prospective investors and new miners arrived to seek their own fortune. By 1849, miners had learned of the big strikes in the West. Many town residents and miners pulled up stakes and headed for California, where opportunities seemed greater.

The rush to California meant the end of any substantial gold mining in Goldville and Arbacoochee or at any other mining sites in Alabama. The miners took with them money they earned from local mining and a wealth of experience. They possessed survival skills in a hostile environment, making them leaders in the goldfields of California. They joined thousands of miners from all walks of life, from farmers to doctors and lawyers, all struck with "gold fever."

From the Civil War period, there is a story about a Confederate soldier who deserted his unit and returned to his home in Goldville. The Confederate army came looking for him. When they found him, they hanged him on a huge tree limb in the center of town as a lesson to others on how deserters were punished. Well into the twentieth century, people reported encountering a headless horseman riding the back roads. Locals believe the ghost of the Confederate soldier is riding the countryside looking for the men who hanged him. Now, only one or two stores mark the center of the old gold mining camp once inhabited by thousands of people. Even the huge tree on which the soldier was hanged has been destroyed. Only the name of the town remains to tell people passing through that once thousands of people lived in the little town of Goldville. A few miles away, in Lineville, the Alabama Gold Mining Camp welcomes amateur miners, their families and friends to stay a few days in the cabins and enjoy panning in the nearby streams.

Hog Mountain (Hillabee Mine, Hogback Mountain)

In 1839, James C. Johnson discovered gold at Hog Mountain, located four miles from Goldville. Using primitive tools, he dislodged a large rock and hauled it to Hillabee Creek in an ox-drawn wooden cart. Finding the site productive, he bought the property in 1842. Millions of rocks were formed at the same time the Appalachian Mountains were formed. Most of the rocks have varying amounts of gold in them. The challenge with mining quartz was retrieving the gold from the hard ore. In the late 1890s, T.H. Aldrich, industrialist and coal mine owner at Montevallo, and his son T.H. Aldrich owned and operated the Hillabee Gold Mining Company. They introduced the use of cyanide in separating gold from rock, significantly increasing the profit from mining. The company was named after the Hillabee Creek below the mountain, where Native Americans had lived and moved their camps regularly along the streams. Miners panned in the creeks before and after the gold rush in the 1840s. The mining company shipped ore samples on the Savanah and Memphis Railroad to the St. Louis mint for evaluation. Traveling by train to Alexander City, inspectors and investors were met by mining managers. The men rode buggies into different mining sites to inspect the mines.

On Hog Mountain, the managers built a pine-slab lodge where the superintendents and investors could stay while they toured the mining site. Others stayed at the Old Russell Hotel in Alexander City. Small cabins were built around the mountain so miners could live close to the mine. Locals

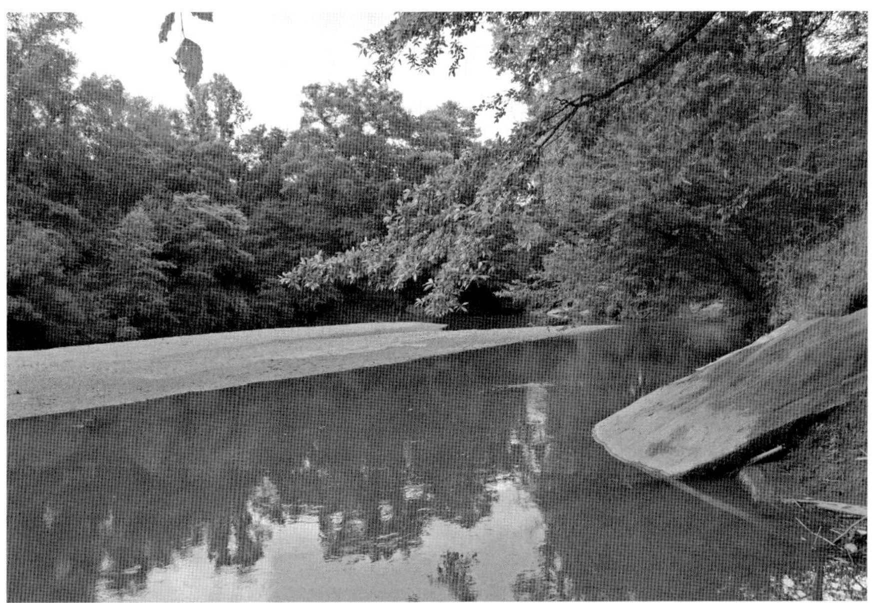

Hillabee Creek. The creek appears the same as it did in the early 1800s, when Indians established towns near the streams. *Personal collection.*

described the site as a "small city." The mining town had electricity years before the people in surrounding areas. Since most of the chemicals used at the mine came from Germany and labor was scarce, Hillabee Gold Mining Company was forced to close at the beginning of World War I.

A revival of interest in gold mining occurred in the Depression years. "Chicken Row," a line of houses remaining from the pre–World War I operation, was repaired and inhabited by miners and their families. Structures at the site included the machine shop, the bunkhouse, the mess hall, the carpenter shop, the assay office, the blacksmith shop, the hoist house, the change house and the large mill house. There was an ore bin where rocks were dumped and a tailing pool. The names of veins identified locations like Main Tunnel, the Red Vein and the Barren Vein; others bore the names of people associated with mining, like the Aldrich vein, the Paisley Vein and the quartz stringers. Approximately two hundred men worked at the mine. They received training in drilling, assaying and other skills that they were able to use after the mine closed and they searched for other work.

Management included Benjamin Russell, director of the board; O.B. Thurlow; F.C. Weiss; and R.M. Fuller, secretary. Mining experts were P.S. Gardener, president and general manager, from Nevada; George M. Brown, vice president and general superintendent, from Arizona; N.O. Johnson, mill superintendent, from Colorado; and Elmer J. Aldefer, manager of the assay shop, from Colorado. With the rise in the value of gold, investors were interested in opening the old gold mines until the Wage-an-Hour law went into effect and investors refused to "sink" more money into the mines. Hog Mountain mine closed in 1946, the same year Alabama received the distinction of producing more gold than any other southern Appalachian state. The largest amount of the gold came from the Hog Mountain mine, which was consistently the top producer of gold in Alabama.

T.H. Aldrich Sr. and T.H. Aldrich Jr. passed ownership of the Hog Mountain property to T.H. Aldrich Sr.'s daughter, Marie Aldrich Cravener. With the closing of the mine, Cravener hired a caretaker and his wife to live on the property and take care of it. They were from the East, where they operated a jewelry business that went bankrupt during the Depression. Mr. Neil built a house elevated above Hillabee Creek and a sluiceway from the house to the sandpile. He and his wife spent a great deal of their time looking for gold.

Dr. Ulrich and His Wine Cellar

Dr. Ulrich traveled from Germany to Tallapoosa County in 1840, when gold mining was at its peak. He and the group of settlers he brought with him stopped in Savannah, Georgia, first, looking for a terrain that would be suitable for growing grapes and making commercial wines. With no success in Georgia, they traveled into Alabama. Dr. Ulrich decided the land near Hillabee Creek was perfect for his purposes. He bought 1,200 acres and dug a large tunnel into the hillside to use as his wine cellar. While digging, he found a vein of gold. He stopped digging the wine cellar and bought equipment to operate a gold mine. He built a wooden stamp mill to process the ore, which he hauled from the tunnel in little cars on wooden tracks. It is not known how much gold he took from the mine. He made the gold into small one-ounce bars and used them to purchase supplies and cattle. Colonel A.H. Moore, an investor, had some of the gold assayed in North Carolina and found it ran twenty-one dollars per ton. Local people thought Ulrich was Dutch, possibly because of the Dutch miners who were digging to find copper near the old gold mining sites. Because the creek had a bend, the location was named "Dutch Bend" and "Ulrich Pits." The land belonged to Robert Russell for many years and remains in the Russell family.

The Devil's Backbone

Many of the old gold mining sites in southern Tallapoosa County are under Lake Martin. Blue Hill, Gregory Hill and Silver Hill were on the Devil's Backbone vein, which ran three miles long and one hundred feet wide. The profit from operating the mines was less than the mining costs, so eventually they were closed.

> *In 1891, state geologist William B. Phillips inspected the Silver Hill mine and reported the mine was currently being operated by Major Parmalee, who later moved the mining equipment to the Gregory Hill Gold Mine and operated a fifteen-stamp mill there. Paralee reported removing $80,000 in gold value out of Silver Hill, Dent Hill, and Gregory Hill at a cost of $100,000. Major Paralee operated mines in the Devil's Backbone District for a decade or more from the early 1880s through the 1890s.*[59]

The Farrow Gold Mine

> *The Farrow mines in the Devil's Backbone District were well known, having been in operation from the 1880s through the early 1920s. Thomas Taylor Farrow established the Farrow Gold Mining Company in the Suzanna community....Located ten miles south of the county seat of Dadeville, the Farrow Mining Company operated for 25 years following the War Between the States. Thomas Taylor Farrow built his own mine machinery, including a self-powered railroad system. Gold produced from the operations was minted in New Orleans, but to earn a dollar profit required spending three.*[60]

Rockford: Gold Mining in Coosa County

In 1835, Rockford was founded on Hatchett Creek. Five years later, the town was selected as the Coosa County seat. Like many other locations in Central Alabama, the soil is rich in minerals, placer gold at Hatchett and Weogufka and lode gold at the Gold Ridge Mine. "Alum Bluff was rich enough in 1840 to keep 50 men working near Hatchett Creek. Other sites include an old pit [that] was sunk within town limits for forty or fifty years. Gold deposits are documented at 'Franklin Mine.'"[61] The Gin House Branch and Carrol and Pole Branches were productive. But primitive methods of mining limited the amount of gold that could be retrieved from the Rockford placer. Miners were quick to abandon sites when they did not yield enough profit to pay for supplies. Hillsides were pocked with open mines that were started and then deserted.[62] Most property now is private. Miners should ask the owners for permission to go on the property and dig for gold. Gaining permission is likely to be as difficult as finding gold.

Construction of Rockford's historic rock jail began in 1825 and was completed in 1842. Designated as the oldest stone jail in the state, the building now serves as a museum and is listed in the National Register of Historic Places. William M. Goggans served as sheriff of Coosa County from 1911 to 1915. He and his two deputies—George Gosdin from Goodwater and Tom Tippit from Richville—maintained law and order for approximately four years. The prisoners received treatment like the prisoners in Andy Griffith's

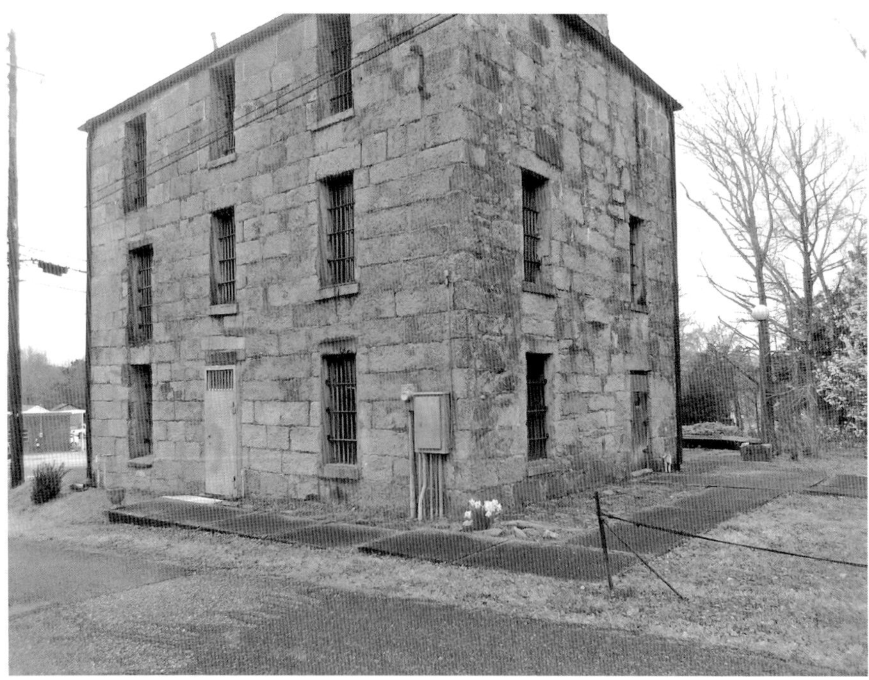

The oldest rock jail in Alabama is in Rockford, Coosa County. It is now a museum in the National Register of Historic Places. *Personal collection.*

Mayberry jail, tended by Don Knotts. Like Aunt Belle, Mrs. Goggans had a kind spirit. She prepared three meals a day for the prisoners. They ate the same food the Goggans family did—eggs and sausage or ham for breakfast; vegetables, cornbread and a meat for lunch and dinner. Sheriff Goggans had a Colt .38 revolver, which survived for more than one hundred years and, on last account, remains in the possession of a family relative. The last person to be hanged at the jail was Charlie White, who killed Dock Maxwell. Sheriff Goggans tried without success to have Charlie's conviction and execution commuted. Mrs. Goggans sewed the black hood Charlie wore for his execution. Charlie stood in the window before his execution and told an audience of citizens who came to the public event, "All that women and whiskey had put him where he was and appealed to the crowd to avoid sin and meet him in heaven."[63]

ALABAMA'S COAL MINING PIONEERS

Coal was one of the first ores to be utilized by Natives and by de Soto and his conquistadors as they explored the interior of Central Alabama. De Soto's chroniclers' narratives described creeks, forests and de Soto's encounters with Native Americans. The chroniclers recorded the bloody battle at Mabila, in which thousands of Native Americans were killed. In the chroniclers' journals, little mention was made of the "smiths" who traveled with the eight hundred or more conquistadors and kept their weapons sharp. They also built pots, other cooking utensils and tools necessary for surviving in the wilderness. The first tent, according to Pickett, to be put up by de Soto's soldiers was the one for "artisans to temper the steel of the Spanish swords and to repair the Spanish arms and armour as the *adeartado* and his men tramped through the wilderness."

Ethel Armes wrote an exhaustive history of coal mining in Alabama. Beginning in 1798, the narrative reveals the location of Alabama's first blacksmith shop, the Indian village of Took-au-batchee, Mississippi (current site of Fort Toulouse). By 1801, the federal government had built a smithy at Fort St. Stephens, site of Alabama's first territorial capital. Two years later, the government built a depot to store iron supplies. Often the blacksmith's shop was the first building to be constructed in a town.[64]

Indian agent Benjamin Hawkins records how he sent a crew of blacksmiths to the Creek Nation "in lower Mississippi Territory." With this crew and members of Andrew Jackson's brigades, the men were "the pioneer coal diggers and iron makers of the state." The early blacksmiths' work was essential to settlers for survival in the wilderness. Settlers needed axes to chop down trees for building homes and to split and stack firewood to heat the home and cook food. Pioneers learned to create and maintain farming tools. They "shoed" horses and mules. They learned to make wagon tires, bolts, fire tongs and plow stocks for outside work. Armes reports that "the earliest use of the Alabama iron ore itself was…to shoe the horses of Andrew Jackson and his men."[65]

OLD TANNEHILL FURNACE

Founded in 1830, the old Tannehill Furnace was a small plant for smelting iron. During the Civil War, Tannehill was expanded into three blast furnaces capable of producing twenty-two tons of pig iron daily to meet the Confederate army's military needs. At the close of the Civil War, Tannehill Furnace and many other blast furnaces were damaged or destroyed. The Tannehill ironworks preceded the Birmingham Iron and Steel District.

> *The remains of the furnaces, among the best preserved in the South, are the centerpiece of the 1,500-acre Tannehill Ironworks Historical State Park, created by the Alabama Legislature in 1969 as a memorial to the state's early iron industry.…The furnaces are listed on the National Register of Historic Places and the Civil War Discovery Trail. The site also has been designated an international landmark by the American Society for Metals.*[66]

In addition to the museum displays of authentic nineteenth-century iron industry, the park has a cotton gin, pioneer farm and working gristmill; more than forty-five historical buildings; and activities available for the visitors.

The remains of the iron smelting furnaces at Tannehill Ironworks Historical State Park constitute one of the oldest industrial sites in the Birmingham Iron and Steel District. In 2017, Tannehill Ironworks was one of six Birmingham historical sites that organized to create the Birmingham Industrial Heritage Trail to celebrate the area's significance in Alabama's industrial and economic history. The Iron and Steel Museum of Alabama, which was opened at the park in 1981, is a southeastern regional interpretive

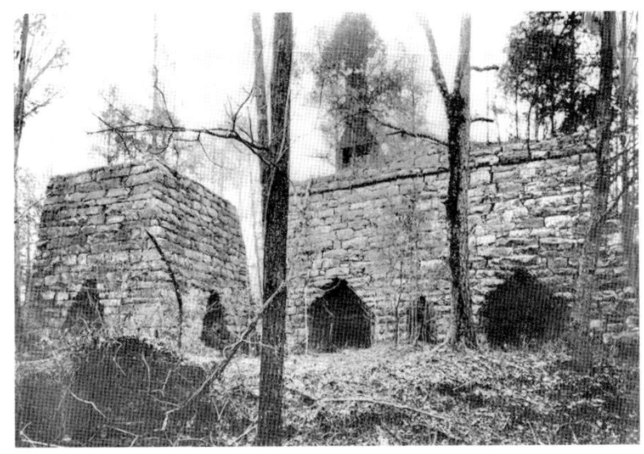

Tannehill Iron Works. Established in 1830, the small plant expanded into a large battery of three blast furnaces to fill the need for weapons during the Civil War. *From James Bennett, "Tannehill Ironworks."*

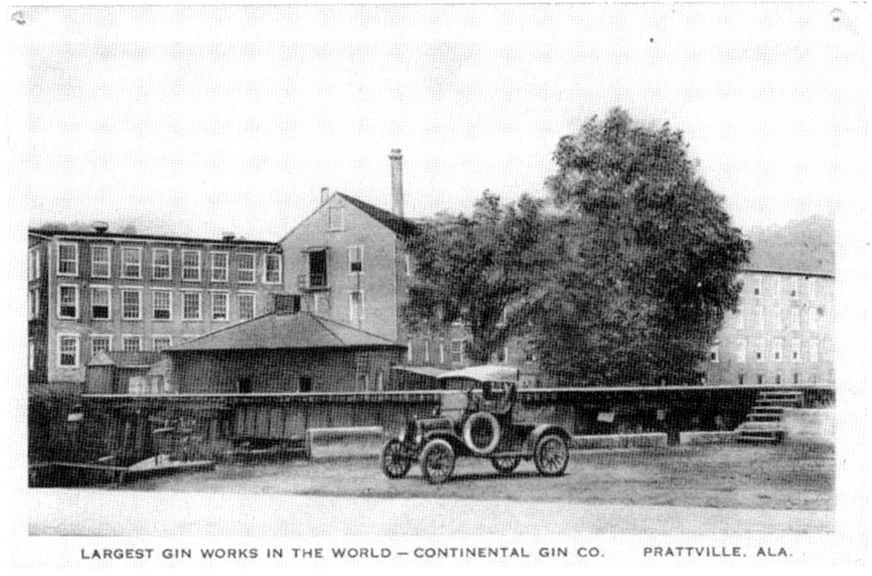

LARGEST GIN WORKS IN THE WORLD — CONTINENTAL GIN CO. PRATTVILLE, ALA.

Created in the 1830s, the Daniel Pratt Gin Factory made Prattville the world's leading producer of cotton gins and made Daniel Pratt Alabama's first industrialist. *"Ghosts of Industrial Past," Tripadvisor.com.*

center that describes how iron was manufactured in the nineteenth century. It contains more than ten thousand relics, including rare machinery from the Tredegar Ironworks in Richmond, Virginia, and collections from the Henry Ford Museum and the Washington Navy Yard. In addition to the Iron and Steel Museum, the site consists of more than forty-five historical buildings—including a large collection of log cabins from the nineteenth century, the John Wesley Hall Gristmill and the May Plantation Cotton Gin House.

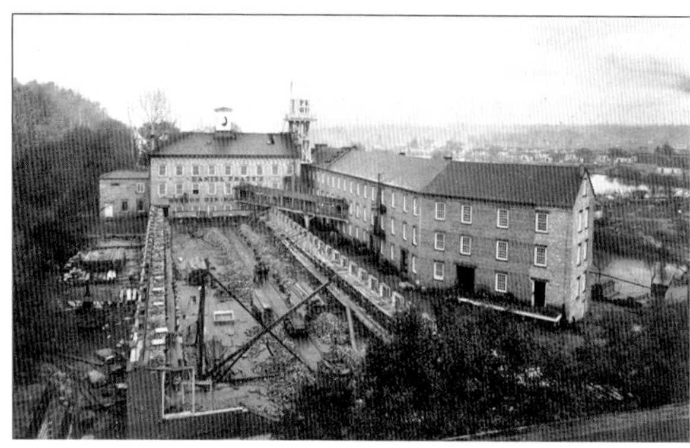

Pratt Cotton Gin reportedly is haunted by a lady in black who took her life after her son Willie Youngblood fell and died. *Alabamabackroads.com.*

Ironically, many small farmers in the area were barely getting by, unaware of the expanse of minerals sometimes just inches below their digging. Rich planters were also more interested in cotton, corn and livestock. The red and brown rock outcroppings, which Indians had used for war paint and for staining implements, were mere inconveniences to farming. Most early white settlers had considered the ore good only for dyeing clothes.

Herbert Jim Lewis described Daniel Pratt in the Encyclopedia of Alabama as Alabama's first industrialist. In 1833, the Daniel Pratt Gin Factory was built in Prattville by Pratt. The factory became famous as the world's largest cotton gin. Pratt also built the town that bears his name and served as a model for future mill towns, providing homes for workers, churches and free schools. Pratt also established a cotton mill and a woolen mill.

Pratt Coal and Coke Company

In 1878, mining industrialist Truman H. Aldrich and James W. Sloss formed the Pratt Coal and Coke Company and built the Birmingham and Pratt Mines Railroad to transport coal within the Birmingham Iron District. Mining communities were built to attract more labor from farms and kept the workers close to their jobs. They were small cities with family homes, stores, schools, churches and recreational and social events. The pay was regular but made in scrip, accepted only at the company stores. The high rate of workers in the convict-release system was legal, but once they were in the system, the convicts' sentences could be extended indefinitely. Mine disasters took the lives of many workers. In 1911, the Banner Mine Disaster left 128 miners dead. Out of this number, 125 were

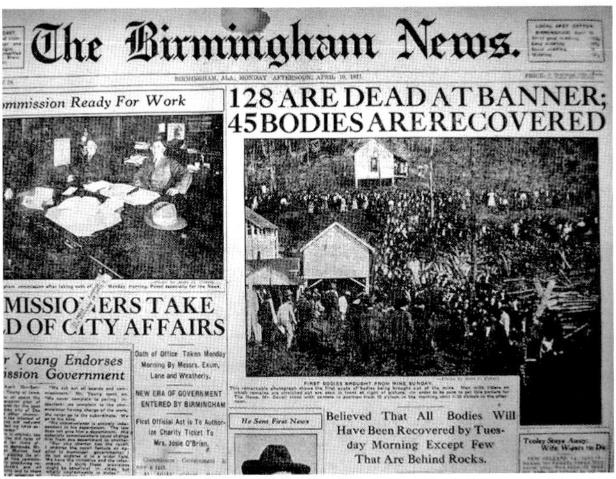

The Birmingham News.

BIRMINGHAM, ALA., MONDAY AFTERNOON, APRIL 10, 1911

128 ARE DEAD AT BANNER; 45 BODIES ARE RECOVERED

FIRST BODIES BROUGHT FROM MINE SUNDAY.

Believed That All Bodies Will Have Been Recovered by Tuesday Morning Except Few That Are Behind Rocks.

He Sent First News

ommission Ready For Work

MISSIO[N]ERS TAKE [...]D OF CITY AFFAIRS

r Young Endorses [...]ission Government

Oath of Office Taken Monday Morning By Messrs. Exum, Lane and Weatherly.

NEW ERA OF GOVERNMENT ENTERED BY BIRMINGHAM

First Official Act is To Authorize Charity Ticket To Mrs. Josie O'Brien.

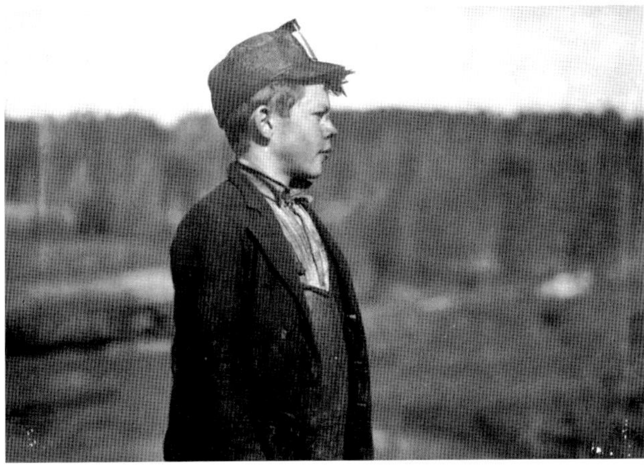

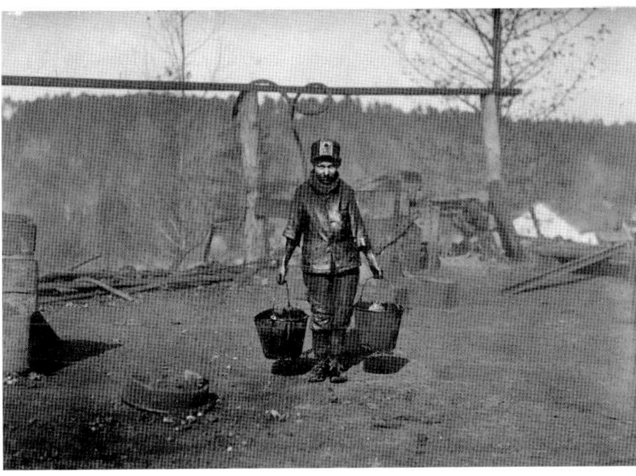

Top: "First bodies brought from mine Sunday. Forty-five bodies are recovered. 128 are dead at Banner." Birmingham News, *April 10, 1911.*

Middle: Alabama was the last state in the nation to officially end the use of child laborers in coal and iron factories. *Lewis Hine/Library of Congress.*

Bottom: Dave, a young laborer, a "greaser" at Bessie Mine in Alabama, 1910. Legislation against child labor was not passed until 1938. *Library of Congress.*

convicts, leased to the Pratt Coal and Coke Company. After the Banner tragedy, the legislature passed a mine safety bill, and Governor Emmett J. O'Neal signed it. "Alabama was the last state in the nation to officially end the practice"[67] of using convict labor.

In 1875, industrialist Truman H. Aldrich purchased the coal mining community and surrounding mines near the present town and college of Montevallo. He named the community, the mines and the post office after himself. Later, he contracted the mines and property to his brother William, who leased convicts to work in the mines. He built a prison to house them and a guard house. The prison was used from 1913 to 1928. A small cemetery was on the property. An equally egregious practice was the use of child labor in the mines. Community members worked in the mines too and lived in Aldrich. The Montevallo Coal Mining Company officially closed on July 5, 1942. Farrington Hall was named for Aldrich's son Farrington, who died of typhoid fever "after cleaning one of the coal mines reservoirs and is said by locals to haunt the structure."[68]

Sloss Furnaces, One of the Most Haunted Places in Alabama

One of Birmingham's leading industrialists, James W. Sloss, built his first furnace in 1882 and began producing pig iron. As the market demand for pig iron lessened, Sloss turned to the production of iron and steel. From 1881 through 1920, Sloss Furnaces produced iron in Birmingham, causing great growth in the city and earning the titles the "Magic City" and the "Pittsburgh of the South." Sloss Furnaces produced iron for nearly ninety years, contributing to the rise of Birmingham. During the late 1800s to early 1900s, many workers experienced horrible deaths, and they reportedly haunt Sloss Furnaces today. In 1872, furnaces began working at top speed, employing immigrants, Blacks and farmers who were in desperate need of jobs with regular pay. Convicts from work-release programs also worked at Sloss Furnaces. Single men lived in crowded barracks, housing up to thirty men. Families could rent a two-bedroom house with yard space for family gardens. Sloss quarters were near the furnace so men could be called to work at any time. There were no breaks or holidays. The men worked a sixteen-hour day for seventy-five cents to one dollar in temperatures as high as 115 to 120 degrees.[69] Wives took in washing and performed other domestic work

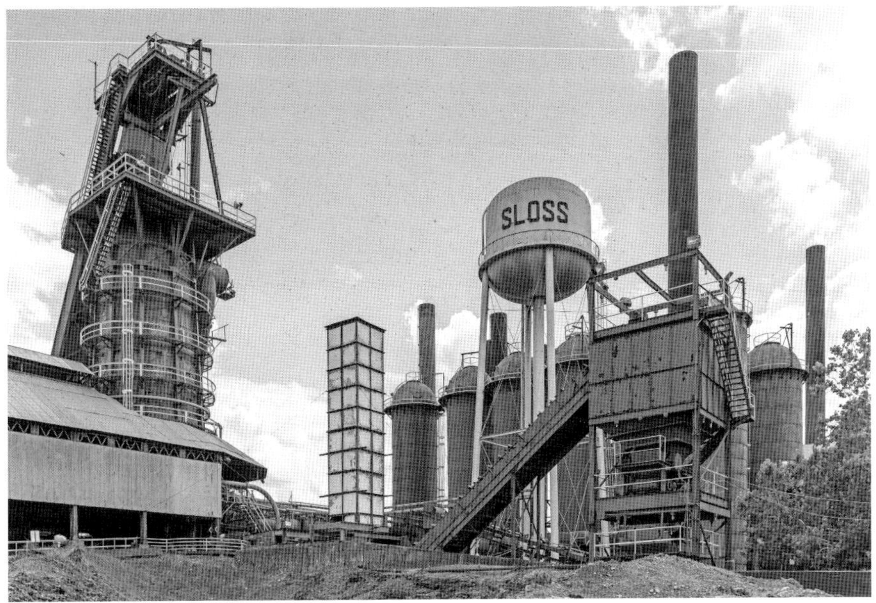

Sloss Furnaces, one of the most haunted places in Alabama. It is in the National Register of Historic Places. *Marker by Alabama Historical Commission. Wikipedia.*

to supplement the family income. The communities had a company store, a school and a church.

Working conditions were described as "a living hell," and the reigning devil was James "Slag" Wormwood, supervisor of the graveyard shift. Forty-seven men were killed when they were working under Wormwood, ten times more than other shifts. Due to fatigue, many accidents occurred, killing or disabling the men involved. The death of Wormwood was especially horrible. He fell from the highest blast furnace into melted iron ore. The mystery around his death was never solved. Some believe the men he had treated so brutally pushed him.

Stories of paranormal experiences people have reported include an orb appearing at the furnaces at night and a creature that chased and terrorized a night watchman. Another man was pushed against the wall and heard a voice telling him to get busy "pushing steel." The evil spirit that appeared to workers and visitors is believed to be that of Wormwood. Paranormal societies have visited the Sloss Furnaces and reported seeing an orb they described as "angry energy." Many believe the spirits of the workers who labored and died under brutal circumstances haunt Sloss Furnaces. In 1971, Samuel Blumenthal, the night watchman for the graveyard shift, was

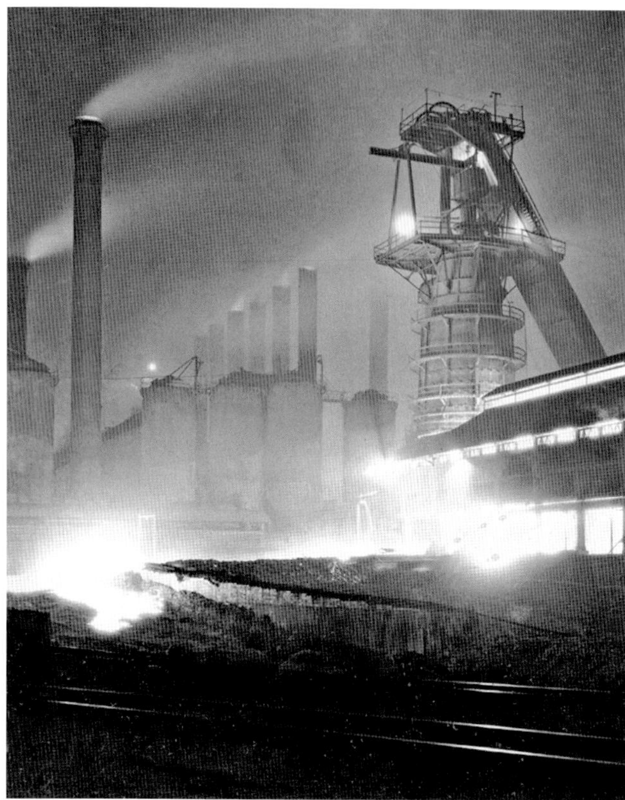

A night image of Sloss Blast Furnaces in operation in the 1920s. Colonel James Withers Sloss founded the Sloss Furnace Company. *Courtesy of Birmingham Public Library Archives.*

conducting his final walk-through of the plant when he came face to face with a monster. Injured in the encounter, Blumenthal rushed to the hospital with a severely burned back. The cause of the burn was a mystery.[70] After being released from the hospital, Blumenthal was too frightened to return to Sloss Furnaces. The stories about James "Slag" Wormwood have now become urban legends.

Sylacauga: Alabama's Marble City

Long before Europeans came into Central Alabama, Shawnee warriors made arrowheads from chips of marble in Talladega County. In 1814, Dr. Edward Gantt discovered marble as he traveled with Andrew Jackson near Sylacauga. Gantt served as the hospital surgeon for the Tennessee Militia during the War of 1812.

All that remains of Gantt Village that was built for the workers and their families are the nearby marble mines. At one time, the town had several stores, two churches, a school (built in 1917) and a lighted tennis court. Gantt had separate quarters for white and Black workers. Black students attended school in a one-room building and used less well-maintained books than their white counterparts. Both groups had their own ball teams and played competitively with other teams. The business sold groceries and merchandise, like boots and gloves. Purchases were charged, and payment was deducted from workers' pay each Friday. The company provided community activities like barbecues and decorating for Christmas, which included placing a Christmas star high atop the water tower, making it visible throughout the village. The children had several activities that kept them engaged. One of their favorites was possible when a train transported loads of marble and returned empty; then they could board, ride the train and play games.

The four managers of the plant built homes on the elevation above the quarry. The town had all the necessities workers might need. The company store was run by Hyman McClure in the 1940s. A post office with a front porch was located behind the store, where the postmistress, Regina Harris, lived in a single room. The tiny building served the community, not just as a post office but as a health clinic and a library. As the population of the village moved to nearby towns, the Gantt post office was moved to Sylacauga, where it is located behind the Comer Museum and Arts Center on Broadway Avenue.[71]

Dr. Edward Gantt moved to Talladega County in 1849 and purchased large amounts of land ceded by the Creeks in the Treaty of Cusseta. In partnership with other investors, he developed a marble quarry. Gantt spent the rest of his life working with quarries and the marble industry. After his death in 1867, the George Herd family purchased several quarries, including the Gantt quarry, near Childersburg and Sylacauga. They built the quarries into a successful enterprise in the 1830s and sold the first quarried marble in 1838. The most common use for the marble was building tombstones, primarily for customers in Talladega and surrounding counties. The Civil War slowed the growth of the prospering marble business when Wilson Raiders burned the buildings at the mining town. Gantt never recovered from the losses and died of an illness in Italy in November 1867. The demand for marble increased near the end of the century when Neoclassical architecture regained popularity. Three major mining companies are in operation today:

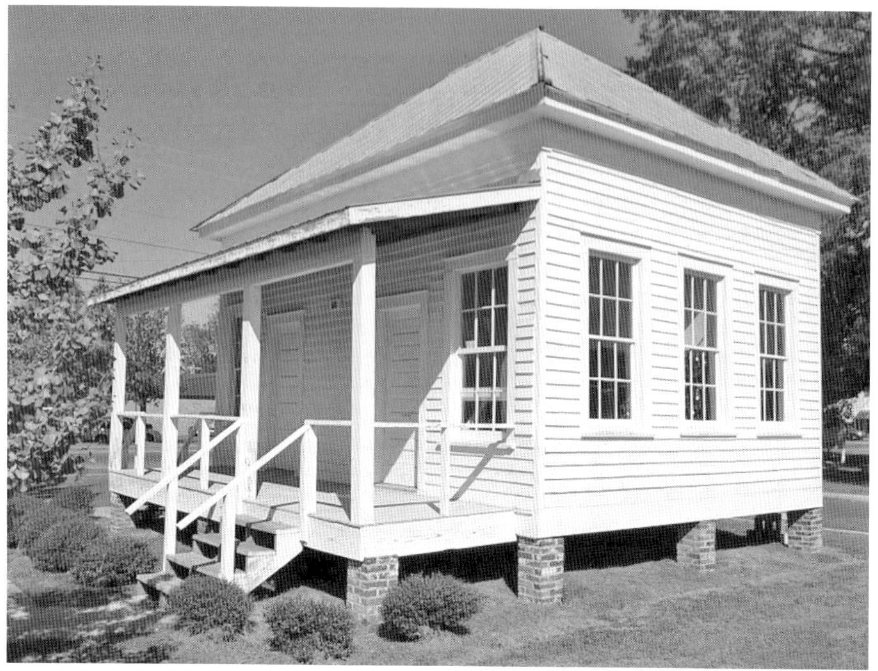

Above: The small post office at Gantt Village was removed from the lot and placed behind the Comer Museum and Arts Center. *Comer Museum and Arts Center.*

Opposite, top: Broad Street, Sylacauga. People dressed formally with top hats and riding 1906 horse-drawn carriages through town on dirt streets. *Pursell files.*

Opposite, bottom: Two workers operate equipment to polish marble slabs at the Gantt's Quarry near Childersburg. The Alabama Marble Company donated marble to many state commemorations. *Pursell files.*

Omya, Sylacauga Marble Mining and Canadian Polycor Company. Ruth Beaumont Cook preserved the history of Sylacauga's marble industry through extensive research and interviews with local families, some of whom had family members who worked at the quarry and lived in the Gantt Quarry community. In 1910, Gantt became an incorporated town and home to mine workers and their families.

The Alabama legislature recognized Alabama marble as the state rock in 1969. Sylacauga is known as "Marble City," where the annual marble festival has been held since 2009. During the ten-day event, sculptors from around the world can work with an Italian master sculptor. Visitors observe and tour the three local quarries. There are sculptures for viewing and some available for purchase. "I've been told there's enough marble there for sculpture and

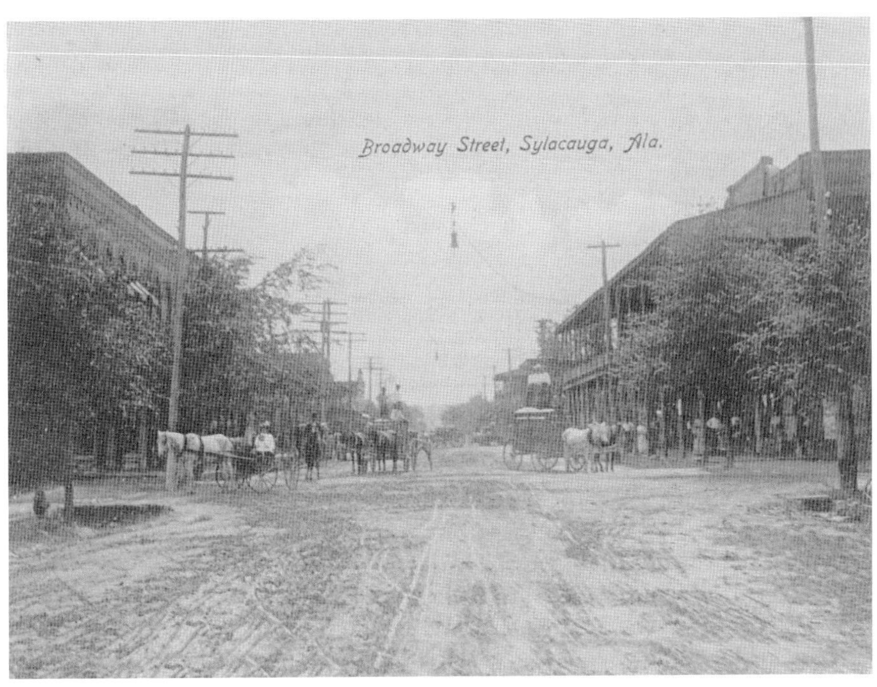
Broadway Street, Sylacauga, Ala.

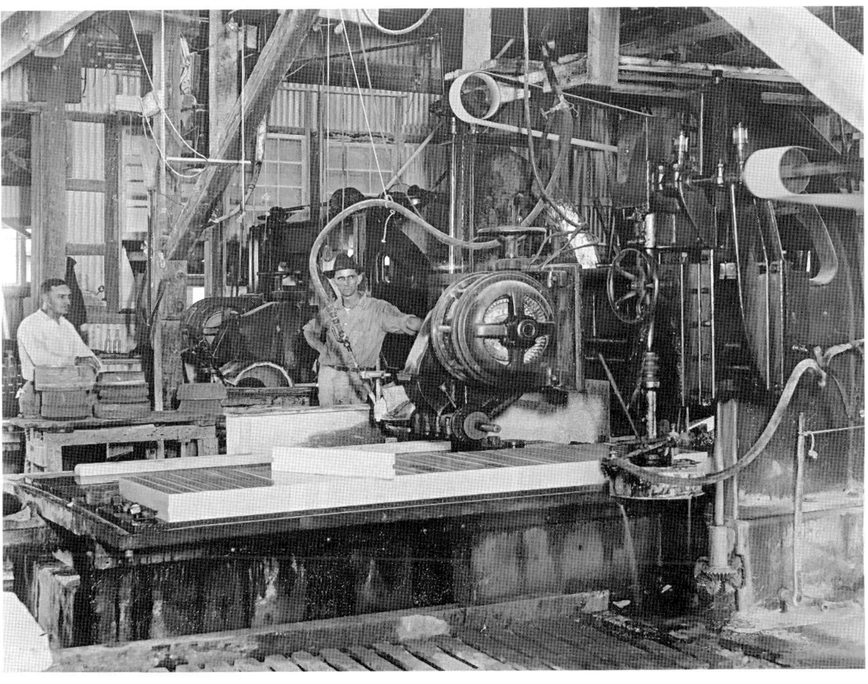

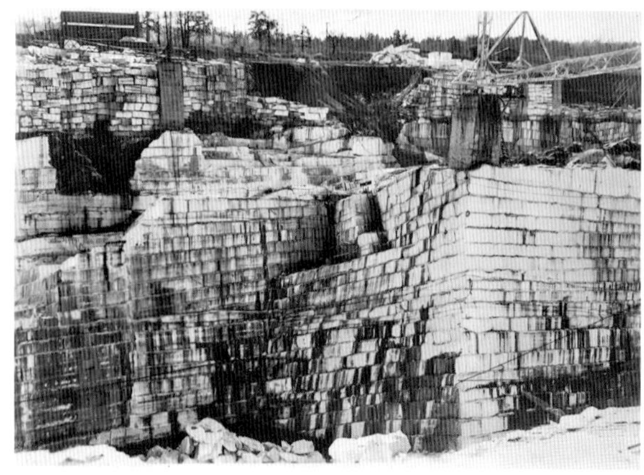

Sylacauga marble is the world's whitest deposit, thirty-two miles long, one and a half miles wide, with a depth of more than six hundred feet. *Alabama Department of Archives and History.*

industry for at least another 200 years," Cook said. "The vein of marble is 35 miles long, a mile and a half wide and goes down quite a ways—300 or 400 feet, I believe. It's a very valuable resource."[72]

Alabama marble is known the world over for its quality. The translucent tone is admired in sculptures and prominent buildings internationally. Among the most famous work of Giuseppe Moretti is the statue of the *Vulcan* on Red Mountain, the largest cast-iron statue in the world. Vulcan is the Roman god of fire and forge and represents Birmingham's iron industry. "*Vulcan* is dedicated at the [1904] World's Fair in the Palace of Mines and Metallurgy and christened with water from the Cahaba River. *Vulcan* won the Grand Prize in the mineral department at the Fair; Moretti also won a medal." The work was admired and awarded the grand prize in the mineral department at the St. Louis World's Fair. Moretti's *Head of Christ* won a silver medal. Continuing his work with marble, Moretti closed his New York studio and moved to Monte Pinos near Talladega, where he worked until his health failed. In 1925, he sold his interest in the Moretti-Harrah Marble Company and returned to Italy, where he continued his work until his death in 1935.[73]

> *The figure was cast from pig iron at Sloss Furnaces between March 10 and April 16 at Birmingham Steel and Iron Company, under the direction of Moretti and company president James R. McWane. During the casting and molding process, members of the Commercial Club's Vulcan Committee raised funds by assembling the plaster cast. It was the first time* Vulcan *was raised in its entirety, and the club charged 10 cents to view it and sold 12-inch bronze replicas.*[74]

One of the changes made to the "Iron Man" was to add a cone-shaped torch that burned red when an accident fatality happened and green if there were no fatal accidents. The lighted torch drew the interest of people while adding a note of caution to drivers. In 1999, the statue and the park underwent a major renovation. After repairs and some recasting by Robinson Iron, the *Vulcan* was returned to its position on Red Mountain overlooking the city of Birmingham.[75]

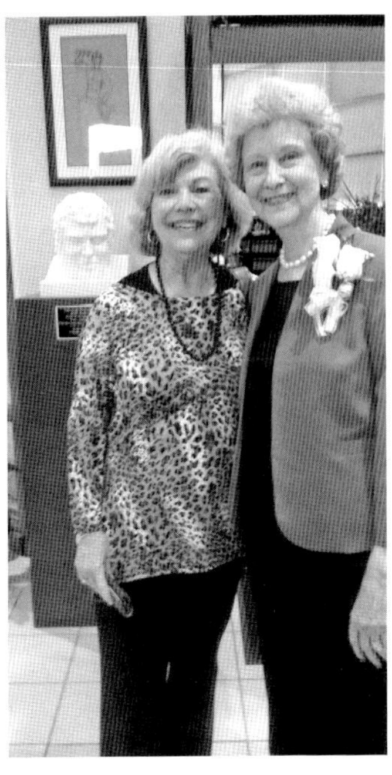

Left: Ruth Cook, author of *The Sylacauga Marble Story*. Director Dr. Shirley Spears retires after thirty-three years of service at the B.B. Comer Memorial Library. *From the* Sylacauga News.

The Falling Star sculpture displayed in front of the Sylacauga municipal complex honors Ann E. Hodges and the phenomenal event of her being struck by a meteorite on November 30, 1954. As she lay resting on her sofa, the 12.21-pound meteorite fell through her living room ceiling, striking her on the side and hip. Stephensport, Kentucky sculptor Don Lawler created the sculpture in honor of Ann Hodges, the only confirmed instance of a person known to have been hit by a meteorite.[76] The fragment, composed of ordinary chondrite, caused a giant bruise on Hodges's side and hip. Michael Reynolds, a Florida State College astronomer and author of the book *Falling Stars: A Guide to Meteors & Meteorites*, stated, "Think of how many people have lived throughout human history. You have a better chance of getting hit by a tornado and a bolt of lightning and a hurricane all at the same time." The Sylacauga police chief confiscated the black rock and turned it over to the U.S. Air Force, which identified it as a meteorite. Opinion as to who should possess the meteorite favored Ann since she was the one struck by it. Not everyone shared this belief though. The Hodges family were renters, and Birdie Guy, the landlady, claimed that since she owned the house that was struck by the meteorite, it belonged to her. Eventually, a settlement was reached in which she was paid $500 and forfeited her claim that the meteorite was hers. Ann said, "God intended it for me. After all, it hit me!" Once confirmed as the owner of the rock, she donated the meteorite to the Museum of Natural History in 1956 so the

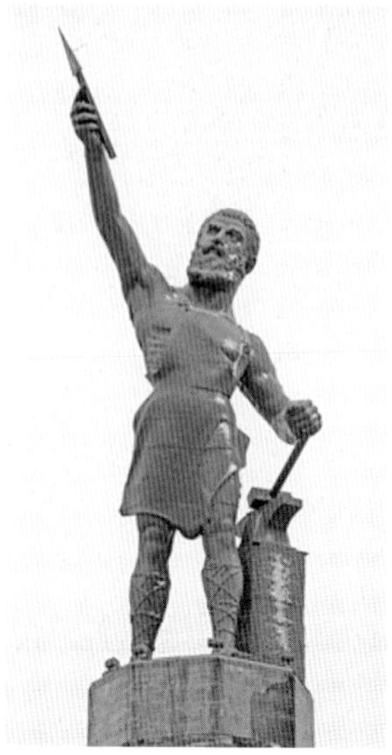

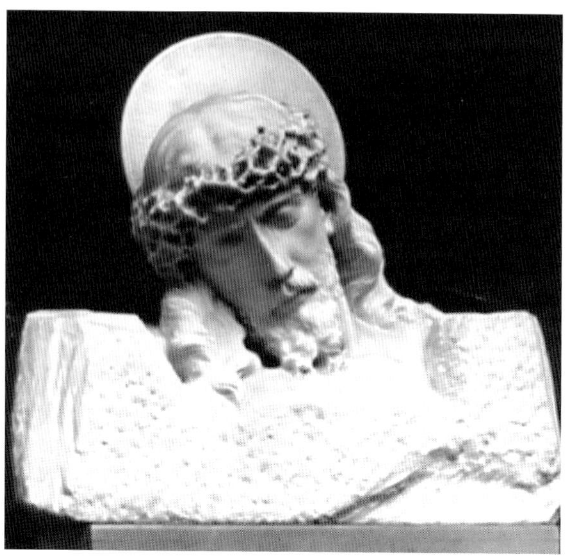

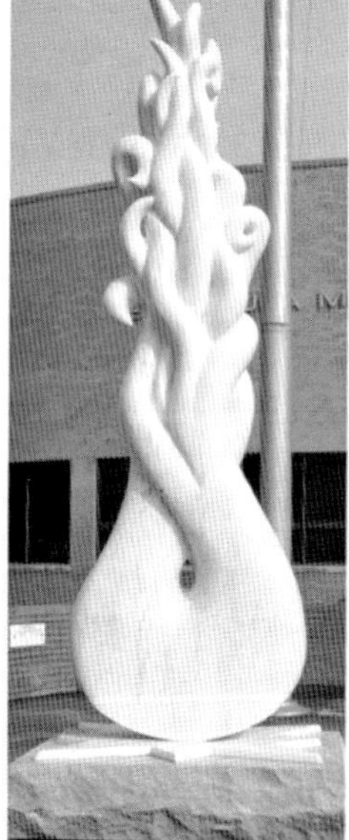

FALLING STAR

Sculptor Don Lawler from Stephensport, Ky.

Lawler came to Sylacauga to purchase marble. While he was in Sylacauga he heard the story of the Hodges Meteorite and was inspired to commemorate the event with this piece. It can be seen at Sylacauga City Hall.

Above, left: The *Vulcan* was constructed in 1903. It is the largest cast-iron statue in the world at a height of fifty-six feet. *Wikipedia.*

Above, right: Moretti's *Head of Christ* sculpture. In 1904, it received a silver medal at the St. Louis World's Fair. *digital.archives.alabama.gov/digital/collection/photo/id3506.*

Left: Sculptor Don Lawler created *The Falling Star* sculpture honoring Ann Hodges, the only known person to be hit by a meteorite. *From Ruth Beaumont Cook,* Magic in Stone: The Sylacauga Marble Story.

public could view it. Due to all the public attention from the meteorite hitting her, Ann Hodges had a nervous breakdown. She and her husband, Eugene, separated in 1964. She never recovered from the deluge of attention that surrounded her and the meteorite story. In 1972, she died of kidney failure at a local nursing home.

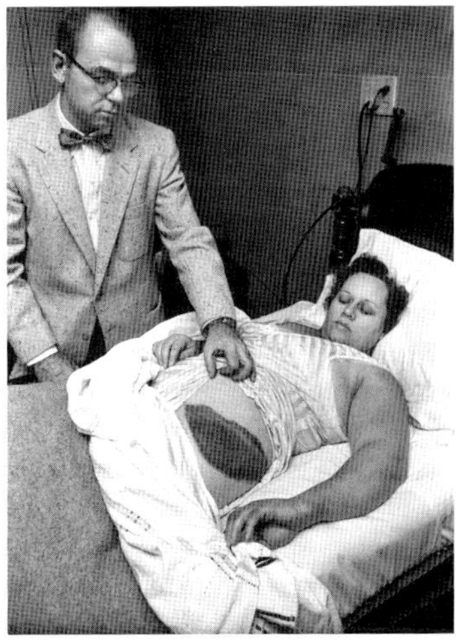

The first person to be hit by a meteorite. Composed of ordinary chondrite, the 12.21-pound fragment caused a giant bruise on Mrs. Hodges's side and hip. *Alice George, Smithsonianmag.com, November 26, 2019.*

Ann Hodges's story is utterly unique in that she was the first person known to have been struck by a meteorite. However, the event was not the first account of heavenly bodies falling from the sky in Alabama. The Leonid Shower of 1833 sent thousands of luminous bodies shooting across the sky; some came near the earth and exploded. The shower of meteors is referred to as "the night the stars fell over Alabama." Articles, books and songs have been written about the Leonid Shower of November 12–13, 1833. People became repentant over ways they cheated or otherwise wronged people as they looked at the sky lit up with stars and meteors falling all around them. Those who owned slaves thought it was Judgment Day, and they apologized to their slaves for selling their families and told them where they were. Bibles were opened and prayers offered to what many believed to be an angry God.

Childersburg: America's Oldest City

Childersburg is located fifteen minutes (10.4 miles) via U.S. 231 N/U.S. 280 W from Sylacauga. The central part of Alabama was home to the great Creek Nation. Coosa (Cosa, Coca) was situated on the east bank of Talladega Creek northeast of Childersburg in Tallapoosa County. Many residents believe the city dates to the Coosa village, a part of the Coosa Indian Nation located near Childersburg. The city claims to be the oldest continually occupied city in America and offers support for the claim.

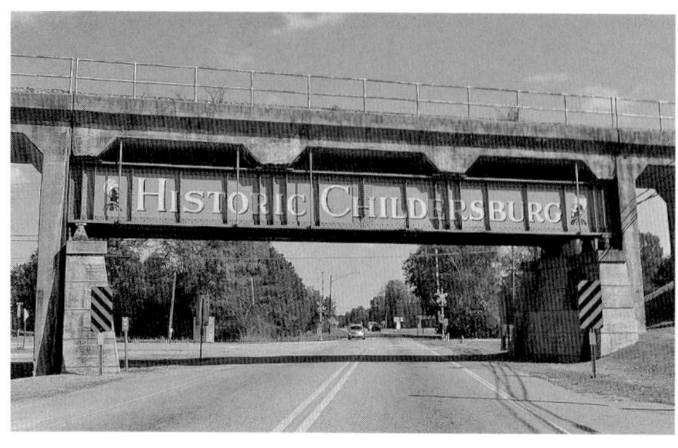

Historic Childersburg sign on the overpass, Highway 280. *Wikipedia.*

> *The cave was known to Native Americans during the Woodland Period; and in 1965 archeologists from the University of Alabama discovered a 2,000-year-old Native American burial site there that held the remains of five individuals. In 1723, an Indian trader from South Carolina named I.W. Wright spent a few nights resting in the cave during his travels through the area. During his stay, he carved "I.W. Wright 1723" into a rock wall in the cave, and these are the oldest graffiti to be found in any U.S. cave.*[77]

De Soto and his men planned to explore the internal Southeast. They ravaged the land they passed through, killing many of the Native Americans, taking their food supplies and making slaves of the captured. "The Spaniards entered Alabama along the Coosa River and followed it to Talisi, which is most likely to have been located near present-day Childersburg, according to historian Charles Hudson's widely accepted reconstruction of De Soto's route. They then headed west along the Alabama River."[78]

THE BIG CAVE

Located in the foothills of the Appalachian Mountains, the Desoto caverns are believed to be the "first recorded cave system in the United States." First named the Kymulga Cave, meaning "old Shawnee town and cave," the name was changed to De Soto Caverns, hoping to increase commercial appeal in the twentieth century. Archaeological research inside the cave unearthed proof that Indians lived in the Childersburg area and at one or more times inside the cave. In 1995, archaeologists discovered the remains of five bodies from two thousand years earlier.

> *DeSoto Caverns formed in Cambrian-Ordovician dolomitic limestone deposited about 500 million years ago; the cave itself is only about 3 million years old. In addition to the central room, a number of small natural tunnels lead off into the substrata for short distances but there is no vast network of caves. Natural formations in the cave include stalagmites and stalactites, rock curtains and draperies, columns, flowstones, and onyx formations. A natural waterfall once flowed in the cave, but it was replaced with an artificial waterfall after the original dried up.*[79]

"De Soto's army left at least two Spaniards here when they departed for Mauvilla (Mabila): a sick black man and a white man named Furada. These two men became the first black and white settlers in the territory now known as Alabama."[80] The date "1723" and initials "I.W. Wright" were carved on the cave wall by a trader from Charleston, South Carolina. An unsupported but interesting story about Wright's death comes from the Native Americans' belief that Kymulga Cave was sacred. For this reason, one of the bodies found in the cave is believed to be Wright's and was left there by the Natives to frighten visitors who might enter. The cave had different purposes through the years, beginning with Native Americans, who believed the cave to be a sacred Indian burial place. During the Indian Removal in the 1830s, Indians may have hidden in the cave to avoid being sent west. During the Civil War, the cave was an important source of saltpeter (calcium nitrate); the Confederacy used to manufacture gunpowder and hide munitions in the cave. During the Civil War, Confederate army officer William Forney built the historic Kymulga Mill. The mill and Kymulga Bridge survived Union attacks that destroyed

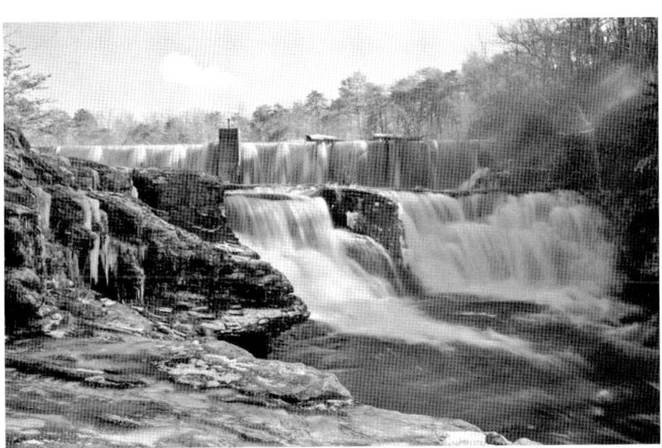

DeSoto State Park on Lookout Mountain is named for Spanish explorer Hernando de Soto and features the 107-foot waterfall near Mentone, Alabama. *www.alapark.com/AL-desoto-falls.*

other structures. Kymulga Gristmill and Covered Bridge were built in the 1860s. The 105-foot covered bridge spans scenic Talladega Creek and lies adjacent to Kymulga Gristmill, which remains in operation. The structures were acquired in 2011 by the Childersburg Heritage Committee, now open to the public as a historic park. The Kymulga Park is listed in the National Register of Historic Places. All fees are used for operation, restoration and maintenance of the park. Attractions include Kymulga Gristmill Covered Bridge, Rainwater Museum and Historical Museum. The park offers campgrounds and cavern tours that include a laser light, sound and water show. Outside amenities include a gift shop, café and picnic area. The cave temperature is sixty degrees. The park offers campgrounds, a maze, gem panning, wacky water golf, archery and more activities.

In the early 1920s, Prohibition was passed, making the sale of alcohol illegal. Illicit sale of alcoholic beverages became a profitable business for bootleggers, who made alcohol available to the public at hidden places. Kymulga Cave was the perfect location, close enough to Birmingham to attract patrons for an evening of entertainment with bands, dancing, gambling and drinking. A rough crowd took over, shooting the ceiling and walls, leaving bullet holes that remain to the present day. As a result, the cave gained the nickname "the Bloody Bucket." The federal agents raided speakeasies regularly and finally raided the Bloody Bucket and closed it.

Businesses in the area began in 1868, with sawmills cutting timber and producing timber products. Scrap wood from the sawmills created fuel for the charcoal business. The fuel was used in the coke ovens of the steel industry farther north. In 1868, the Alabama and Tennessee River Railroad became the Southern Railway. The railroad's arrival promoted Childersburg businesses, making possible the transport of local products to larger markets and the import of merchandise from other cities. Located in the foothills of the Appalachian Mountains, "Alabama's Big Cave" has many attractions besides the caves, including a three-quarter-acre maze known as the Lost Trail Maze and a Christian themed "sound, light, and water show." A favorite activity for visitors is panning for gems. Other attractions are a climbing wall and amusement park–style rides. The tourist appeal continues to grow.

Childersburg was incorporated in 1889, a Talladega County city of about five thousand people. The caverns have been owned by the Mathis family for five generations. In 2015, Ida Mathis began managing De Soto Caverns with the help of other family members. His daughter Joy is now the president and her husband, Jared, is chief visionary officer. They are working with a

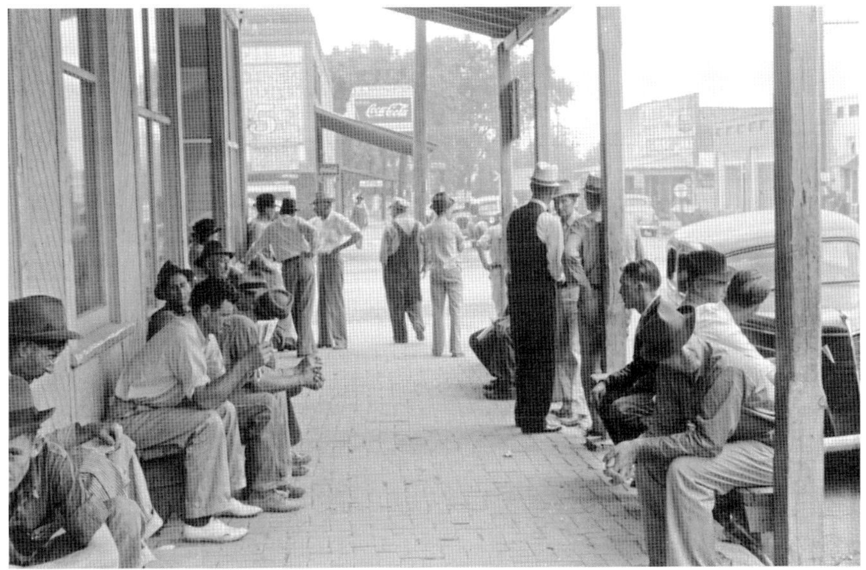

Men from the area and other communities waiting to apply for work in the Childersburg munitions plant during World War II. *Pursell files.*

team dedicated to expanding the current attractions, which include family activities like a maze, mini golf, a climbing wall and a petting zoo.

A high point in Childersburg's history was the operation of a munitions factory during World War II in the 1940s. In addition to employing local people, many came from different parts of the nation seeking employment at the plant. Childersburg and nearby towns like Sylacauga experienced economic booms.

The "High Place"

In Muskogee language, "Chaha" means "high place." Cheaha Mountain is the highest peak in Alabama. The Cheaha State Park first opened to the public in 1933 and is the oldest continually operating state park.

Located in the lower Appalachian Mountain ranges, Cheaha rises 2,407 feet above sea level. A lake with crystal-clear water reflects the colored leaves in the fall. Rocky cliffs offer a breathtaking view of the foliage and trees in the Talladega National Forest. In August 1540, Hernando de Soto and his expedition party tramped through the forests and knelt by a mineral

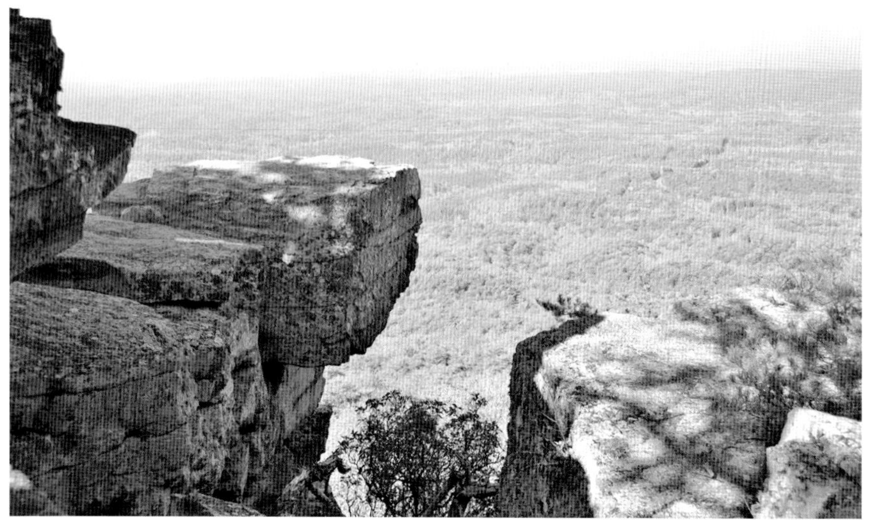

The highest point in Alabama, Cheaha Mountain ("high place"), stands 2,413 feet above sea level in the Talladega National Forest. *National Park Service.*

spring to drink the refreshing water. They had few supplies, mostly the food and weapons they had stolen from the Creek Indians. They foraged villages to take whatever they found to sustain them on their search for gold and other treasures. They found no treasures; ironically, more than two centuries later, white settlers discovered gold in this same region—not an amount to compare with the gold found in the West but enough to attract thousands of gold diggers to the Alabama Gold Belt in the 1830s and '40s. But even the discovery and mining of gold did not match the appeal of the three resorts near the Talladega Mountain: Old Talladega Springs, Clairmont and Borden-Wheeler.

In 1814, one of Andrew Jackson's men was tramping through the forest on his way to join with the Tennessee Militia to fight in the Battle of Horseshoe Bend. Seeing several deer drinking water, he investigated and found a spring bubbling with mineral water. The Indians knew about the spring and used the water for medicinal purposes. The location became known as Talladega Springs and developed into a commercial endeavor as Talladega Spring Resort in the 1800s. Much of the region is named for Native Americans, and myths were created about the origins of the mountain, especially the "lookout cliff."[81]

December 1998
The Sleeping Giant: An Indian Legend—Talladega Co., AL

Many years before the white man penetrated the forests of Alabama, there dwelt a happy, thrifty tribe of Indians in the central portion of the present county of Talladega. The chief of this tribe was the great Choccolocco; a man of vast possessions. He had only one daughter, the Princess Talladega, whom he treasured above all he possessed.

Talladega, as every princess should be, was the most beautiful maiden in all the realm. Choccolocco, realizing that he could not continuously keep Talladega within the walls of his selfish heart and domain, began to cast about for a suitable mate for his treasured daughter.

Now, in those days, as well as in these, one had only to think a thing, and the world anticipated the unspoken thought, and ran away with it. It so happened that great chiefs, mighty and rich, old and young, from far and near, began to make offers of handsome gifts to the stern old Choccolocco for the hand of his daughter. Some found favor in the sight of Choccolocco, but Talladega said: "Nay. Give me time. The right companion will come along someday, who loves the things that I love, and we can be happy wandering through life together."

Time passed on, until one dawn of an April day, Talladega wandered down a winding path to the sparkling spring at the foot of the hill. The world seemed lovely in spite of the scheming father. Suddenly she heard a song in the distance. It was beautiful. The song grew nearer and nearer, and more beautiful, until the singer burst into view, as Talladega dipped her earthen pot into the water. She met the dark eyes of a comely young warrior, and at that moment she knew that in some way their future would be linked together. Thus began, in the spring of that year, an affair which clandestinely grew beyond the imagination of Choccolocco. Each morning a song was answered, a friendship ripened, and a love was strengthened. The wooing progressed, until one day Talladega, approaching her cabin, heard voices. Her name was mentioned. To her dismay she realized that Cheaha, an ugly old chief from an adjoining province, was bargaining with Choccolocco. As she caught the glowering eyes of Cheaha, she immediately knew that she would not submit to wedlock with this eagle-eyed suitor. After Cheaha left, Choccolocco informed Talladega that he was the favored chief, and that she would probably soon follow him to his province. Talladega slept none that night, and soon after dawn she was out awaiting the song of her young lover, Coosa.

It was indeed a sad morning they spent together. Coosa possessed no property, and he was so overcome with the helplessness and pathos of their situation, that he plunged into the woodland, where he wandered up and down the banks of his favorite stream for days. His thoughts were only of Talladega. He could see her reflection in the still waters; hear her voice in the rapids; and to this day the stream that bears her name still echoes the voice, and reflects the beauty of Talladega.

After Coosa had wandered for days, he decided that he could stand it no longer, and he went back to speak to Choccolocco. Coosa found him alone and he immediately stated his business. He told him that he was not a man of property, yet he was young, and taller, swifter and stronger than any warrior of the province; aside from this, he knew where valuable minerals were stored in lands unpossessed, and he would direct Choccolocco to them, whereby he could enrich himself more plentifully than any chief in all the land. In fact, he plead so appealingly, and painted a picture so enticing, that Choccolocco listened with growing interest.

"If you can bring me samples of valuable ores, and assure me of the possibility of ownership," said Choccolocco "I shall consider your proposition more fully."

There was never a happier being since the world began than was Coosa at his hopeful remark. Turning he found that someone else had joined them, and from the scowl on his face, he discerned that this was the erstwhile acceptable suitor, who had overheard the latter part of Choccolocco's remarks.

Cheaha turned without a word. An idea was brewing. He hastened to put it into action. He had brought with him two young warriors, whom he immediately dispatched, one for a famous medicine man of his tribe, and the other to follow Coosa. The medicine man had discovered an herb that would put the strongest of men immediately to sleep, and he could not be aroused until the antidote was administered; that antidote being known to none but the medicine man himself.

Along about nightfall the young warrior who followed Coosa returned with the information that he had pitched camp at the west end of the valley. When Cheaha and the medicine man arrived they found Coosa peacefully sleeping, with arms folded on his breast and his face turned to the heavens. The medicine man stealthily crept to the sleeping Coosa and quickly administered the drug. When he assured Cheaha that the drug had taken the desired effect, Cheaha cruelly turned on the medicine man and killed him on the spot.

In the meantime Choccolocco, becoming disgusted at the delay of Coosa, ordered wedding preparations for Talladega and Cheaha.

Talladega had discovered her sleeping lover, and made many secret visits to him whenever chance permitted. She became so depressed and unhappy as the wedding day approached, that Cheaha decided that it would be wise to tell Talladega that Coosa could never be awakened. Talladega said nothing. She only sat motionless and gazed into space.

When the wedding day arrived, no bride was to be found. The woodland was searched, the hills and valleys scanned, but no bride was to be found. In the midst of the turmoil, an Indian lad burst into the group with the exciting news that Talladega had been discovered, lying dead on the breast of her sleeping lover.

Although the drug was so powerful as to keep Coosa always sleeping, it also carried the power to make him grow, and while lying there sleeping, he has grown through the centuries until the mighty figure has become a great giant, now forming a mountain many miles long, where he can be seen from many roadsides. Mother Nature has lovingly covered him with earth, to protect him from the cold. She has planted trees and shrubs to shield him from the hot summer sun, and she has scattered flowers here and there, and each year birds flock to the Sleeping Giant to herald the coming of Spring. And there he lies, still dreaming of his beloved Talladega, "The Bride of the Mountain."[82]

Early records speak of the mountain also as the "Giant at Rest" and the "Resting Giant."

Chapter 4

MINERAL SPRINGS

In the 1800s, when settlers moved into Alabama, they built homes and established towns near creeks with clean drinking water. They needed adequate water for farm animals and large quantities for crops during dry seasons. In addition to having water for domestic reasons, they needed enough water to operate gristmills, water mills and other industries.

Before the settlers came, the Creeks, Choctaws and Cherokees used water from mineral springs for medicinal purposes. Fresh, clean water was believed to be pure, good or sweet. Often, towns were named for the quality of spring or creek water: Goodwater, Sweetwater, Stillwater, Coldwater, Hotsprings, Warm Springs and Sulphur Springs. Not all water smelled fresh, was clear or even tasted good. Sulphur created a rotten egg smell, and iron added a muddy color to the water. Mineral waters were bubbly due to the gases.

By the late 1800s, enterprising community members had built resorts near mineral springs, and they became rich sources of income for the people who owned them. The resorts attracted people from great distances. Like Talladega Springs at the foot of Cheaha Mountain, other resorts were built near the cool mineral springs in the southern Appalachian foothills. The inns and cabins were exotic retreats with swimming and fishing pools. Chefs from places like New York prepared delicious dishes for patrons, who dined with Birmingham orchestras playing in the background. After the evening meal, guests moved to the outside pavilion and danced well into the night before retiring to the inn or a cabin. Patrons came from as far away as New York to enjoy the therapeutic values of the springs and take part in the resort activities, such as boating.

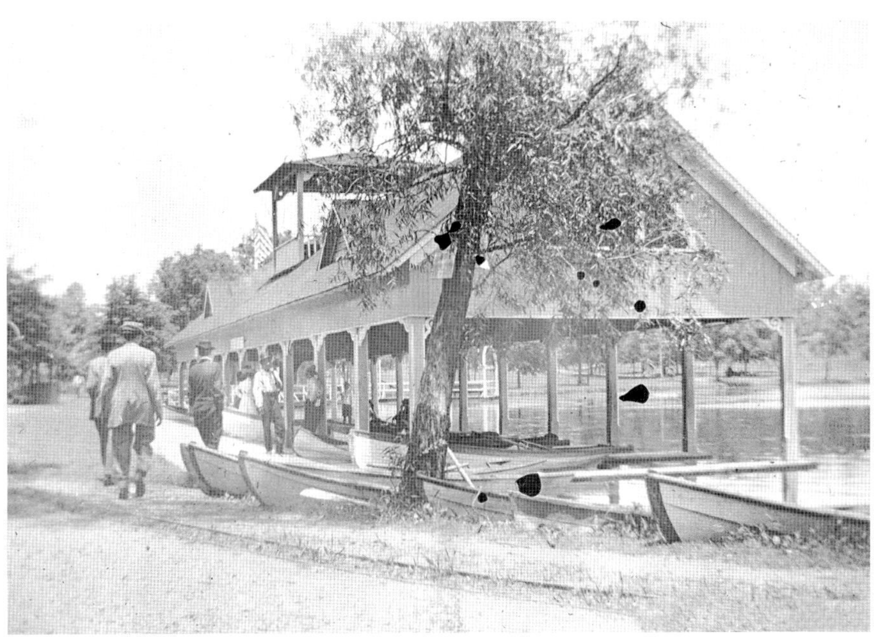

At Talladega Springs, resort guests enjoy boating. An open pavilion allows for boats to be tied and remain on the water. *Pursell files.*

Prior to the arrival of the settlers, Indians knew the location of the Talladega Springs that flowed down Sulphur Mountain. They used the mineral water to heal sicknesses and wounds. In the early 1800s, many of those wounds came from skirmishes of tribes among themselves and later in battles with Jackson's soldiers and the Tennessee Militia. A soldier from a Tennessee unit discovered Sulphur Springs when he noticed deer gathered at a spot, drinking the water. He was on his way to join Jackson's army and allies to fight at the Battle of Horseshoe Bend in the present Tallapoosa County. He relayed his story to other soldiers, so the spring was remembered and visited by others after the war.

Talladega Springs: Built by Water and Ended by Water

Famous for its healing Sulphur springs, Talladega Springs grew from a small town into a bustling resort charming guests from across the country

> *with its boutique hotel, first-class dining and of course, notable Southern hospitality.*[83]

A small community was established near a mineral spring that flowed down Talladega Mountain and created several springs. At this early time in Alabama's history, no one could have imagined the famous Talladega resort town that would develop in the late 1800s. The spring was known first as Sulphur Springs, then as Talladega White Sulphur Springs. The third name, Franklin, was given by soldiers from Franklin, Tennessee, who remained after the Battle of Horseshoe Bend to establish a small farming community. In 1845, the tiny town of Franklin became known as Talladega Springs and over a period of decades grew into a large resort town.

The therapeutic benefits of the mineral spring waters drew patrons from great distances to enjoy the luxuries of the resort town. *The History of Talladega Springs* notes the Louisville and Nashville (L&N) Railroad connects the town to Birmingham, Calera, Gadsden and Anniston, running up "to four times a day and often delivered more than 500 guests each day."[84] Guests stayed at the one-hundred-room, two-story hotel with a grand dining hall, where they were served by waiters wearing formal white coats. The elegant features of the dining hall and famous cuisine compared to popular restaurants in large

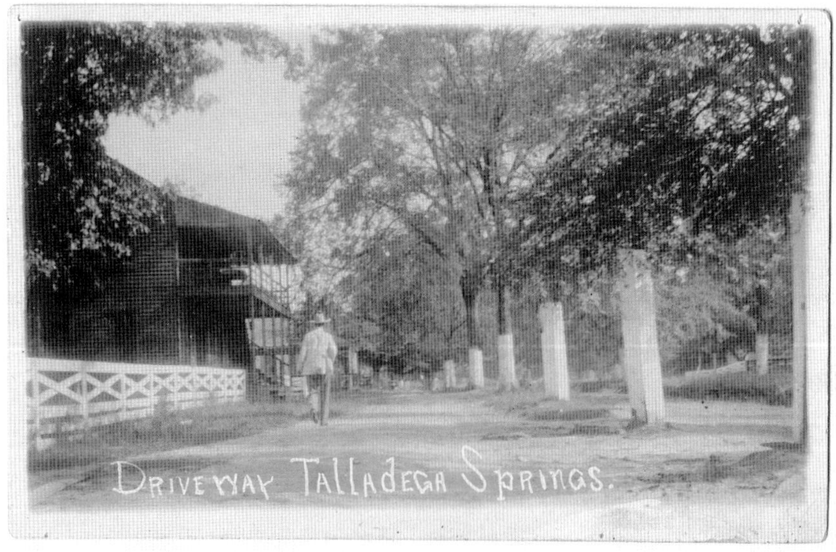

This Talladega Springs postcard depicts smartly dressed man with a panama hat strolling down the sidewalk of Talladega Springs resort town. *Pursell files.*

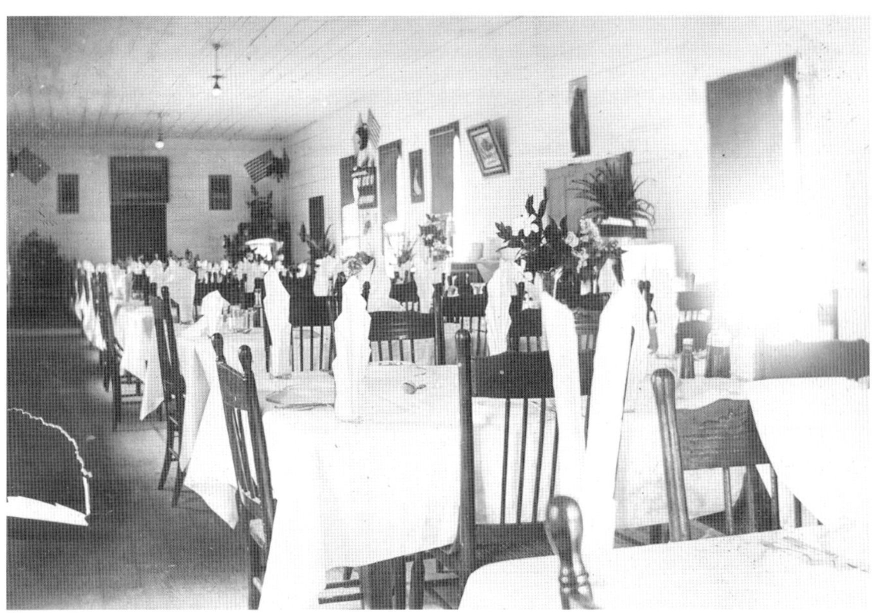

Patrons stayed at the one-hundred-room, two-story hotel with a grand dining hall, which was like popular restaurants in large cities. *Pursell files*.

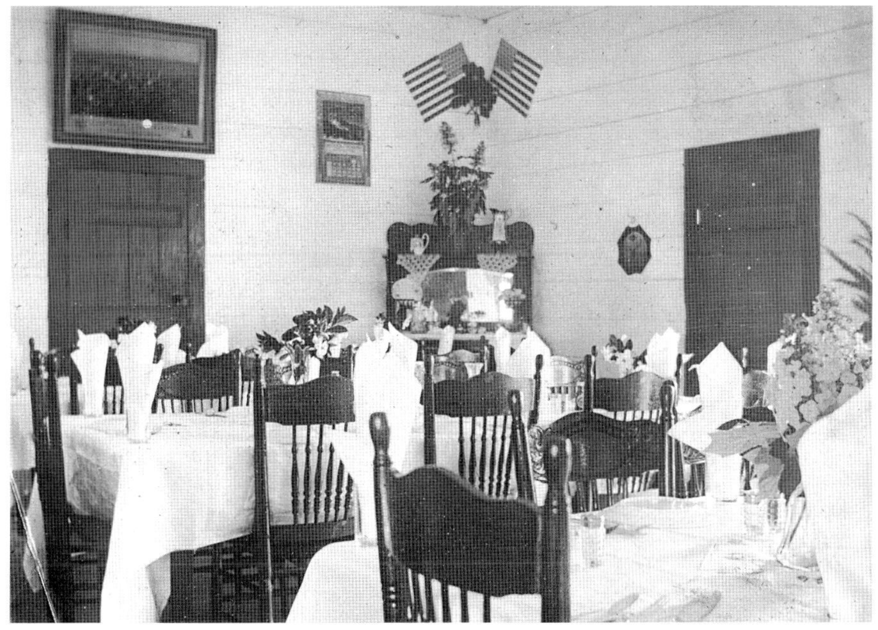

The therapeutic benefits of the mineral spring waters and the amenities and food drew patrons from great distances to enjoy the resort. *Pursell files*.

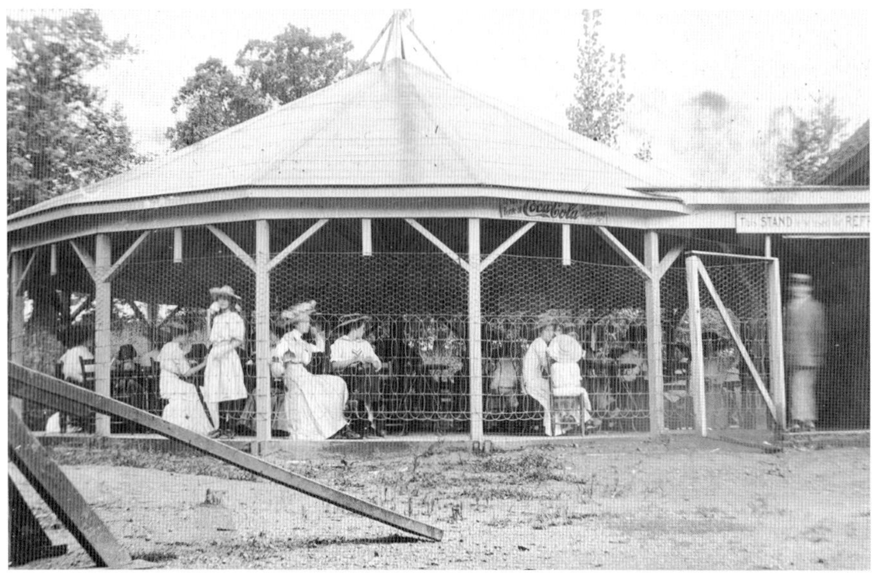

Orchestras from Birmingham entertained patrons at the pavilion while they danced and enjoyed sipping Coca-Colas before retiring for the evening. *Pursell files.*

cities such as New York. Orchestras from Birmingham and Montgomery played dinner music and afterward provided music for dancing at the large pavilion. The Coca-Cola bottling plant brought additional growth and interest to Talladega Springs. An advertisement for the popular beverage was attached to the side of the pavilion.

It must have seemed to the patrons of the resort town that the prosperity would last, but several events altered that belief. The momentum of growth was broken with the construction of Lay Dam. The hydroelectric facility was located a mere fifteen miles downstream. When the water dammed on the Coosa River, the backwaters rose to within a mile of the spring, causing patrons to fear malaria might spread into Talladega Springs. Fear of this fatal disease resulted in the exodus of many patrons.

With the increasing popularity of automobiles and convenience in traveling longer distances, Talladega Springs now had to compete with newer, more modern resorts. Fewer patrons traveled to the resort aboard the Louisville and Nashville Railroad, causing a drastic reduction in the services the railroad could provide. The depot, the mail service and other customer services ceased. What remained of the "Queen of Alabama Watering Places" were the brick swimming pool, the hotel and other amenities that deteriorated from lack of maintenance. Talladega Springs was now a ghost town with a legacy of happy days in the late 1800s and early 1900s, a remarkable time when the L&N Railroad brought hundreds of visitors daily to enjoy the amenities and health benefits of the mineral springs.

The resort began to deteriorate before the Pursell family bought the property and constructed a fabulous new resort they named Pursell Farms. Their purpose was to preserve the history of the Old Talladega Springs and develop a modern resort with a luxurious restaurant overlooking a beautiful green golf course. Several cabins were constructed for rent as well.

"It All Began with FarmLinks"

Jimmy and Chris Pursell founded the Parker Sylacauga Fertilizer Company in 1904. By the end of the twentieth century, Pursell Technologies had revolutionized the agronomy industry and moved to "scenic Pursell Farms."

The Pursell family honors Talladega County's history, beginning with the earliest historical notes about the 3,200 acres and the story of how Hernando de Soto and his conquistadors rode through Talladega, capturing Natives to

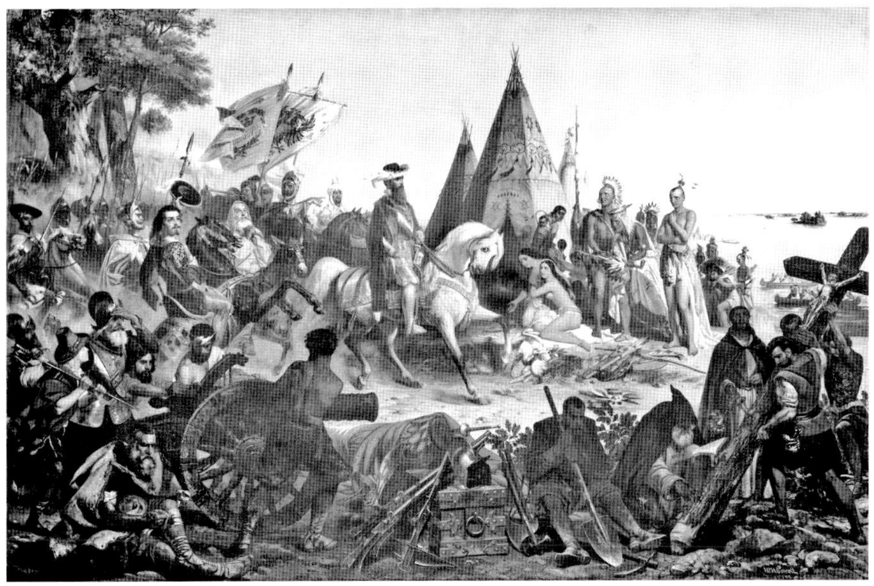

In 1540, de Soto and his conquistadors arrived at Indian villages in present Central Alabama on their way to the interior of the present Southeast United States. *Wikipedia.*

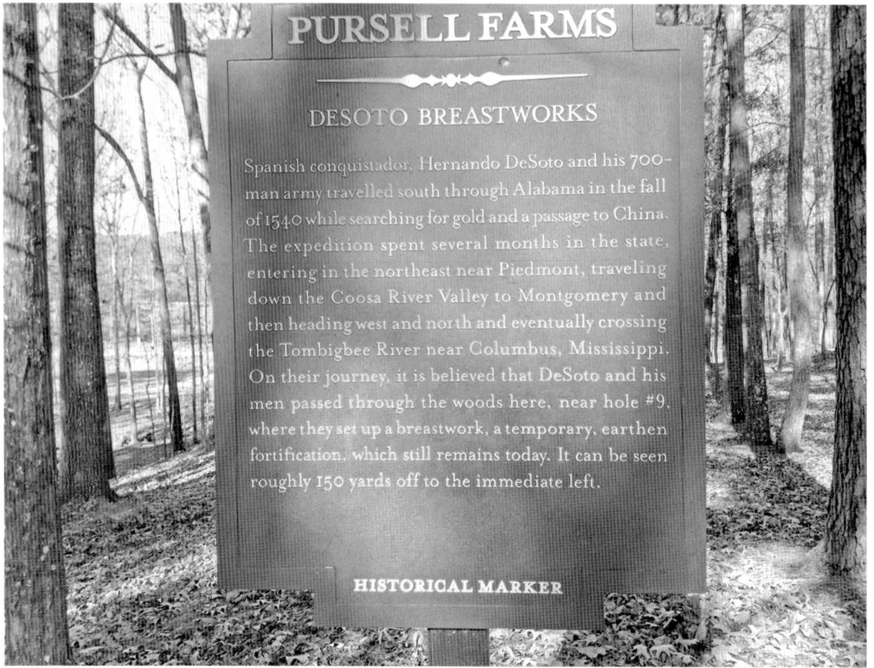

When de Soto and his men passed through what is now Talladega County, they attacked Indian towns. It is believed that they built the breastworks shown by "A Breastworks Historical Marker." *Pursell files.*

serve as slaves and guides and killing many others. When they were finished looting, they burned the villages.

David Pursell, the third-generation leader of the family businesses, stated the company's objectives: "We grow to provide our guests with a superior experience. We honor the family name in all that we do." David was manager of the in-house advertising agency for the family's fertilizer company. Later, David became vice president of sales and marketing for Pursell Industries, and when the company split in 1997, David assumed the role of president and CEO of Pursell Technologies.[85]

David promoted the FarmLinks golf club as a bridge from past to present, shifting from the fertilizer business that began in 1904 "to a premier resort complete with an award-winning golf course, wedding venue, corporate meeting spaces, and the only ORVIS Shooting Grounds in the South."

In 2001, David Pursell began creating a research and demonstration golf course with the goal of improving the golf industry, with FarmLinks serving as a living laboratory for industry leaders.

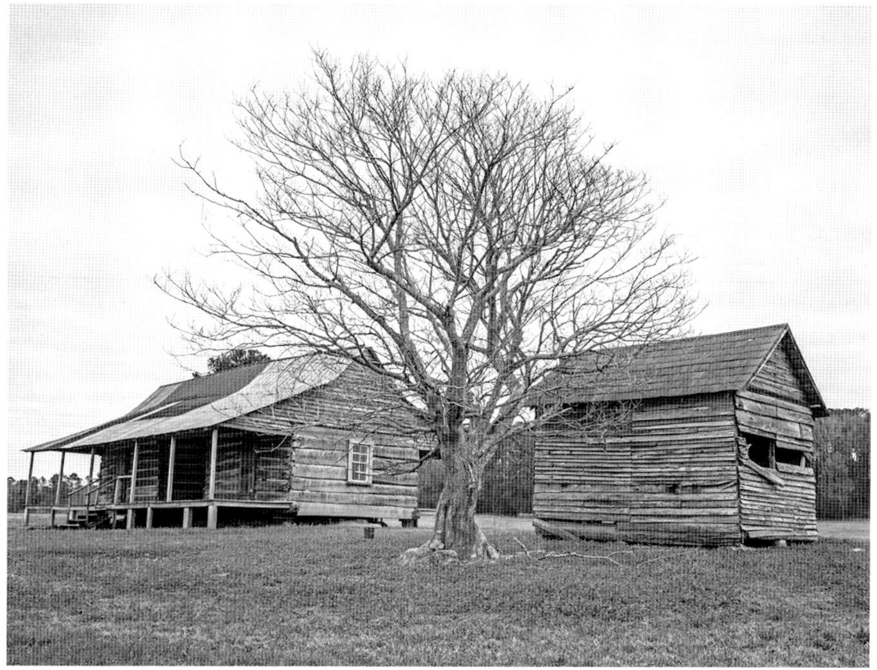

The Robert Hamilton family's old house and field are a part of the old Talladega property, near the Old Talladega Springs. *Pursell files.*

"On June 4, 2003, the vision came to fruition as 550 guests, including family friend, Jim Nabors, and then Alabama Governor Bob Riley, celebrated the official opening of the 7,444-yard, par-72 Hurdzan-Fry designed course, FarmLinks. David currently serves as CEO of Pursell Farms. He is also an accomplished artist and well-known for his pencil portraits of distinguished golfers."[86]

"Third Finger, Left Loaf"

This is not a ghost story, but a story of the lasting friendship between two high school athletes, Jimmy Pursell and Jim Nabors (aka Gomer Pyle from *The Andy Griffith Show*). Jimmy and Jim played on opposing teams when they were in high school. During a basketball game, Jimmy was taken to the hospital with a broken leg. The next day, Jim and students from Sylacauga High School went to the hospital. The visit started a seventy-year friendship and involved shared events in their lives, such as the time Jim Nabors served as Jimmy's best man at his wedding to Chrissy Parker. Jimmy and Jim both lived in California at the time. Jimmy was at Mather Air Force Base in Sacramento, and Jim was in Los Angeles, where he worked for NBC. As the best man, and the only attendant for the groom, Jim was a busy participant. He sang and ushered guests. He was best man and ring holder. In true Gomer Pyle style, he lost the ring. The wedding proceeded without the ring, which was found later. An episode of *Gomer Pyle, U.S.M.C.*, titled "Third Finger, Left Loaf," was based on the real-life event of Jim Nabor losing his friend's wedding ring. In the TV episode, Gomer decided that the ring must be in one of six hundred loaves of bread "he baked in the base mess hall." In honor of his friends and the real loss of the wedding ring, the bride and groom in the show were named Jimmy Pursell and Chrissy Parker.[87]

Jim Nabors got his break in major TV programing when Andy Griffith saw him at a Santa Monica nightclub. The character Gomer Pyle was so popular that Jim had his own series with CBS, *Gomer Pyle, U.S.M.C.* Jim's successes in the entertainment business earned him a star on the Hollywood Walk of Fame.

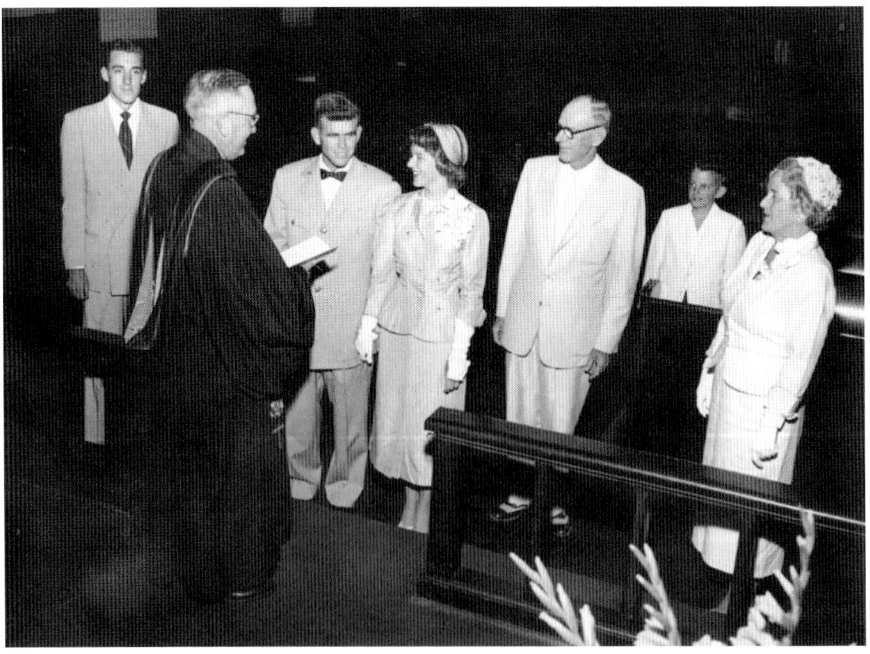

Jimmy and Chrissy Parker's wedding. Jim Nabors was the best man and ring holder for the groom. He also sang and ushered guests. *Pursell files.*

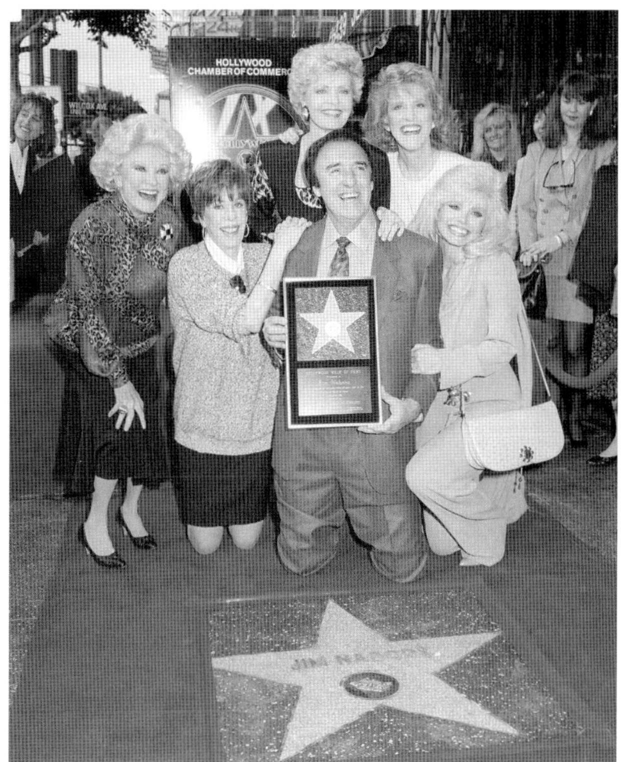

Jim Nabors is awarded a star. He is surrounded by stars: Carol Burnett is on his left, and Loni Anderson is on his right with several others. *Philip Potema, Hollywood Chamber of Congress,* Chicago Tribune, *December 1, 2017.*

At Pursell Farms Resort, pictures in the lobby of Tom's Pub illustrate many events shared by Jimmy Pursell and Jim Nabors, including wedding pictures and a picture of three directors' chairs: Andy Griffin, Don Knotts and Gomer Pyle. Jim had lived in Honolulu since the mid-1970s and had many "treasured items." When David Pursell and his wife, Ellen, visited him, Jim told the Pursells to go through the items and "take what they wanted." They chose the 1903 Brunswick pool table Jim had in his home in Los Angeles. He said, "Everybody that came over to my house ended up playing on that pool table because it was right there in the den: Frank Sinatra, Dean Martin, Sammy Davis Jr., Bing Crosby, Carol Burnett, Lucille Ball, Burt Reynolds, Dolly Parton, Michael Jackson and the Jackson 5." Pictures of the celebrities hang on the wall in Tom's Pub near the "116-year-old" pool table, "with an inscription that reads in gold letters, 'Jim Nabors' Famous Pool Table. From Hollywood to Pursell Farms.'" Jim Nabors's sketch of himself and Sergeant Carter, a gift to his friend David Pursell, is displayed with David's and Ellen's sketches of other famous people. When Jim Nabors visits Sylacauga, he stops to visit old friends. He

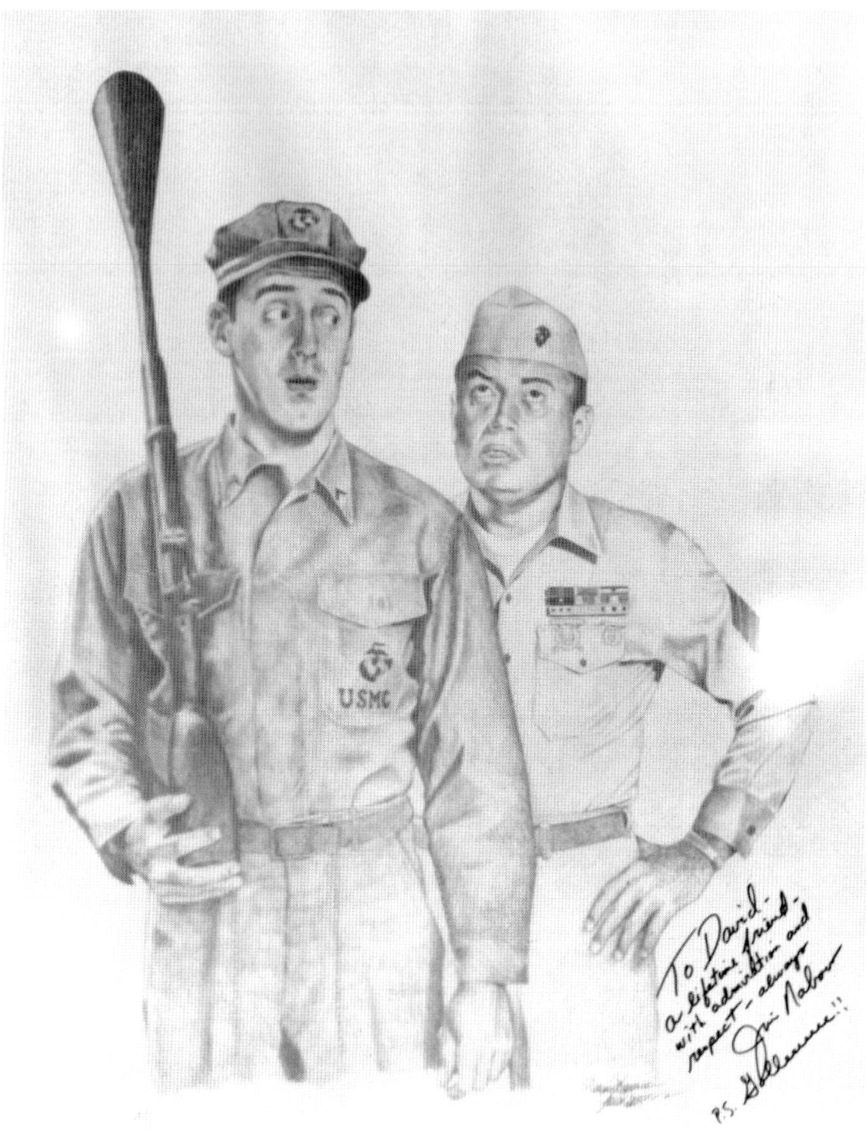

Jim Nabors sketched the picture of himself and Sergeant Carter for his friend and signed it, "To David, a lifetime friend in admiration and respect—always." *Pursell files.*

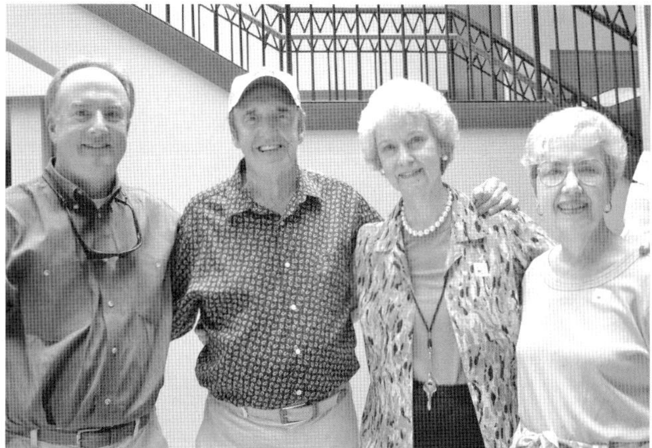

Left to right: Gregg Bolton, Jim Nabors, Shirley Spears and Jo Andrews at the B.B. Comer Memorial Library when Jim was on his way to Texas for his eightieth birthday celebration. *Shirley Spears*.

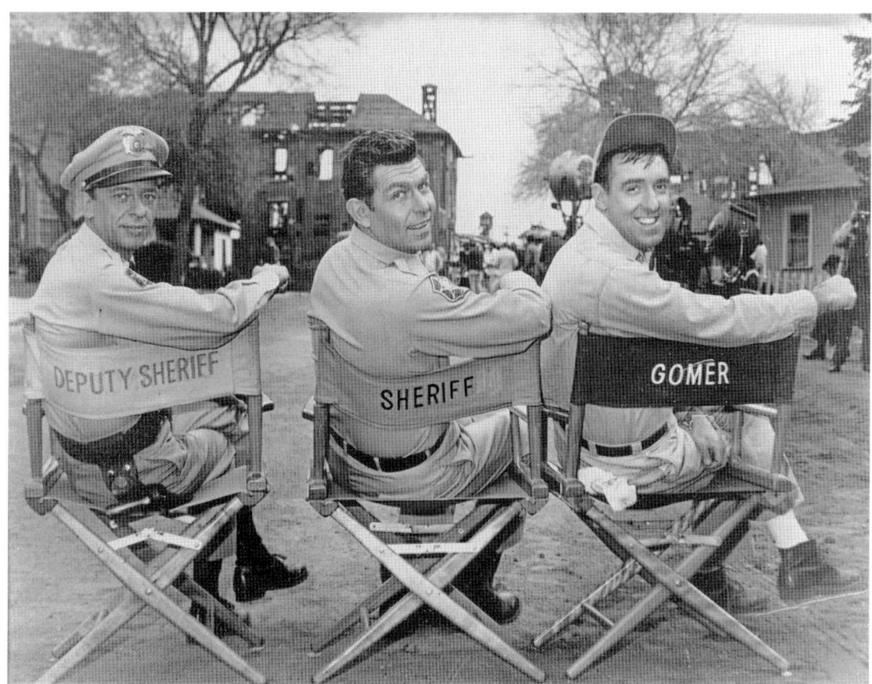

Friends of Pursell's, Nabors, Griffin and Knotts. Jim Nabors became a celebrity on *The Andy Griffith Show*, followed by his own show, *Gomer Pyle, U.S.M.C. Pursell files.*

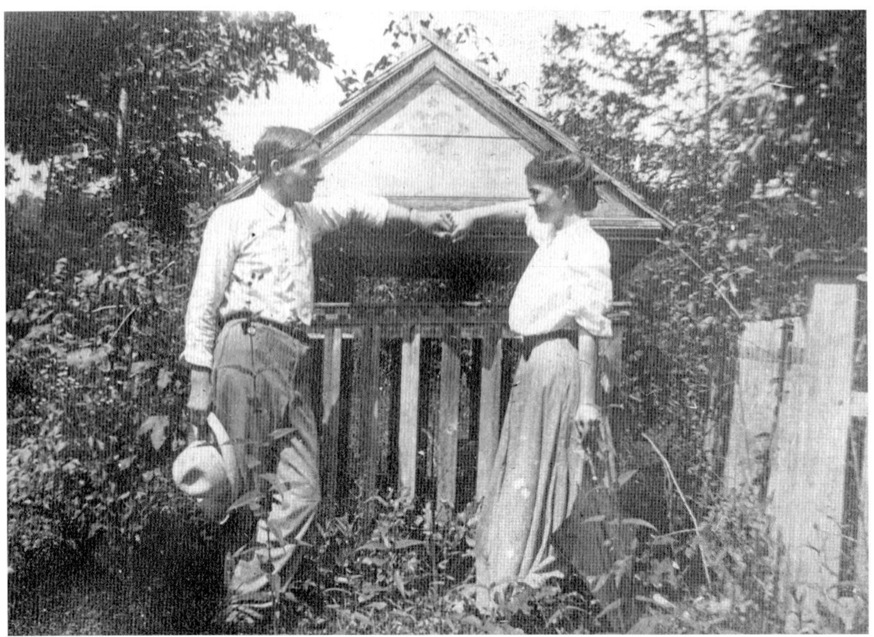

Robert Hamilton and a friend stand by the unknown gambler's tomb, built by other gamblers who felt sorry for the man who lost all his money. *Pursell files.*

stopped at the B.B. Comer Memorial Library on his way to California to celebrate his eightieth birthday with friends Shirley and Ted Spears.

Pictures of the Old Talladega Springs cover both walls of a long hall in the resort, where guests can pause and read captions. The pictures show the Talladega resort in its prime days, including the hotel, pavilion, train depot and other features.

As the name FarmLinks promises, the Pursell resort links the present to the past, with sketches and pictures honoring the Old Talladega Springs resort and more modern pictures painted by David and his wife, Ellen.

CLAIRMONT SPRINGS

In the 1800s, numerous mineral springs were in the foothills of the southern Appalachian Mountains. Clairmont Springs was a health spa located at the base of Talladega Mountain in Clay County. In 1833, George Morgan of Tennessee was the first to own property around Clairmont mineral springs.

He established a farmstead in 1833, three years before the Indians were removed to the West. His son John Tyler Morgan played with the Creek Indian children. John Tyler served in the United States Senate from 1877 until his death in 1907. George Morgan's son-in-law purchased 520 acres of the land. The community became known as Jenkins Springs, where he and his family lived for fifty years. The land was renamed Clairmont Springs, and Morgan developed it as a rambling two-story hotel. Lots were sold for building private cottages. When the eastern railroad valve AM built a line that passed by the resort, people traveled from major cities like Atlanta to enjoy the delicious food Mrs. Jackson prepared. Guests had access to a "recreation hall, swimming pool, dance pavilion, tennis court, a stable of horses, and a five-acre fishing lake."

The owner, the Clairmont Springs Company, ran into financial stress and asked James William Jackson, manager at a small hotel nearby, to take over the hotel in 1911. Jackson was a successful manager and purchased all the hotels owned by the Clairmont Springs Company. The Jackson family operated the hotel for the next sixty-five years. The summer season for staying at the summer resort was June 1 through the end of September.[88]

> *Rates were $2.00 a day, $9.00 a week, or $30.00 a month and included a room, three bounteous meals a day, and access to eleven springs, each with a different mineral composition. When Clairmont Springs closed in 1975, time, weather, and vandalism took their toll. However, the natural beauty of the place remains, and the springs flow as strongly as ever.*[89]

To advertise and provide evidence of the mineral content of the water, state geologist Dr. Eugene Allen Smith was hired to analyze the waters of eight springs. Smith's report was attached to early brochures advertising Clairmont. In its day, Clairmont was known for the healing qualities of the springs. How each spring can have different compositions would remain a mystery were it not for geologists like Dr. Smith and others in the scientific field.

Fruithurst

In the 1800s, settlers came into East Central Alabama looking for rich soil to grow cotton. A few families settled in Cleburne County. Like other isolated farming communities, growth came when a railroad line connected them with larger towns like Birmingham and Atlanta. The community was first named Summit Cut because so much work was required to cut and grade the hills to lay railroad tracks. After Summit Cut, the residents changed the name to Zidonia, from the biblical name Sidon or Zidon, which reflected their inspiration and belief that the town would grow and succeed.

Zidonia became a ghost town when the price of cotton dropped after 1865. Many European textile factories and merchants found more affordable suppliers from outside the South. The cotton prices fell, and farmers had little money to support themselves and provide for their families. Further discouraging to the people, during the Civil War, the Wilson Raiders rode through town, burning buildings and looting the meager resources.

When northern investors came to Zidonia, residents were eager to sell. Most owners gladly accepted the money since they were in dire straits with no income and little future in farming. In *Fruithurst: Alabama's Vineyard Village*, Virginia Voss Pope notes that one of the raiders, C.A. Crawford, returned in 1895 and constructed elegant homes in Fruithurst. The inn was three stories high with eighty rooms and elaborate trimmings. Exotic food was prepared by a cook imported from France.[90]

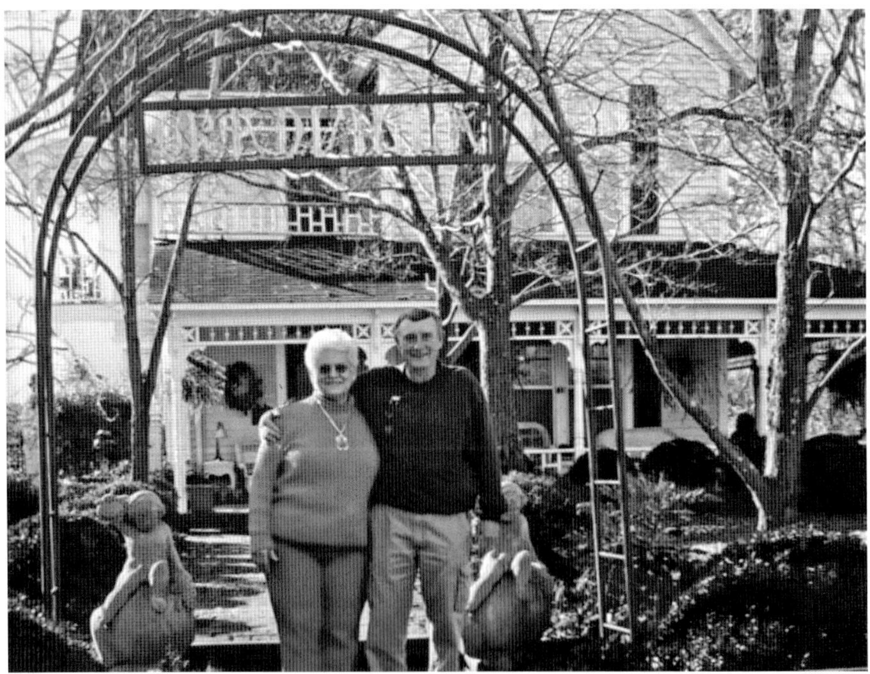

Ralph and Faye Luminack Hilburn in front of their home, the Granvilla in Fruithurst, which once served as an inn. *Personal collection.*

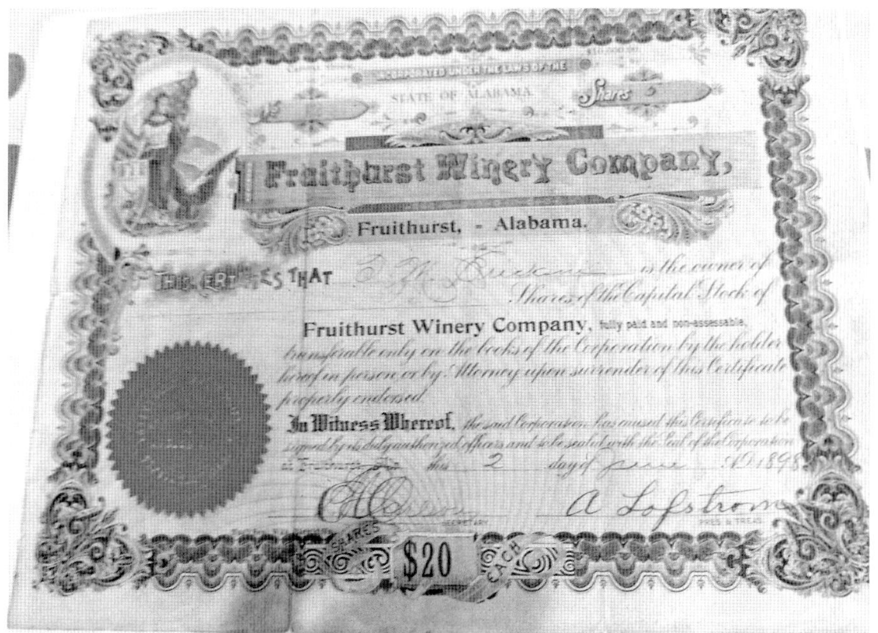
Incorporated under the laws of the
State of Alabama
Shares 3

Fruithurst Winery Company,
Fruithurst, - Alabama.

This Certifies That [illegible] is the owner of [illegible] Shares of the Capital Stock of Fruithurst Winery Company, fully paid and non-assessable, transferable only on the books of the Corporation by the holder hereof in person or by Attorney upon surrender of this Certificate properly endorsed.

In Witness Whereof, the said Corporation has caused this Certificate to be signed by its duly authorized officers and to be sealed with the Seal of the Corporation at Fruithurst, Ala. this 2 day of June A.D. 1898

[illegible] Secretary
A Lofstrom Pres. & Treas.

Shares $20 each

A twenty-dollar certificate for three shares of stock in the Fruithurst Winery Company, incorporated by the state of Alabama on June 2, 1898. *Fruithurst Winery Company.*

The town of Fruithurst was an agricultural experiment incorporated in 1894 by the Alabama Fruit Growers and Winery Association (AFG&W). One member of the investment group was E.B. Hammitt of Springfield, Massachusetts; others were from Illinois, Iowa and Ohio. In 1895, the Swedish Lutheran Church was built. Workers included northern Europeans, Swedes, Danes and Norwegians to clear and cultivate the twenty thousand acres in Fruithurst. Their work was to plant vineyards, grow grapes and establish a winery. In addition to cultivating grapes, other fruits and vegetables were grown.

> *The Fruithurst Inn was the showplace of the town. It claimed to be one of the finest hotels in the South and was justly qualified to make the statement. There were several churches established and several wineries were in operation. By 1898, Fruithurst had become a real boomtown with people pouring into the area. The city was laid out with diagonal streets, joining parallel avenues linking the entire city together.*[91]

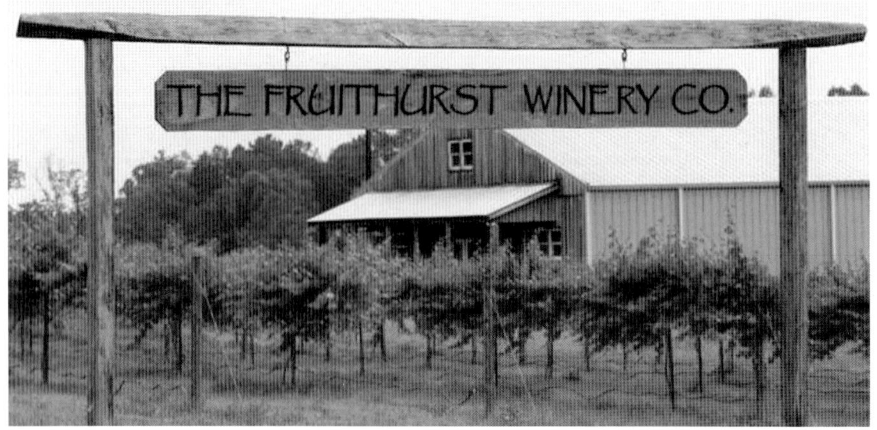

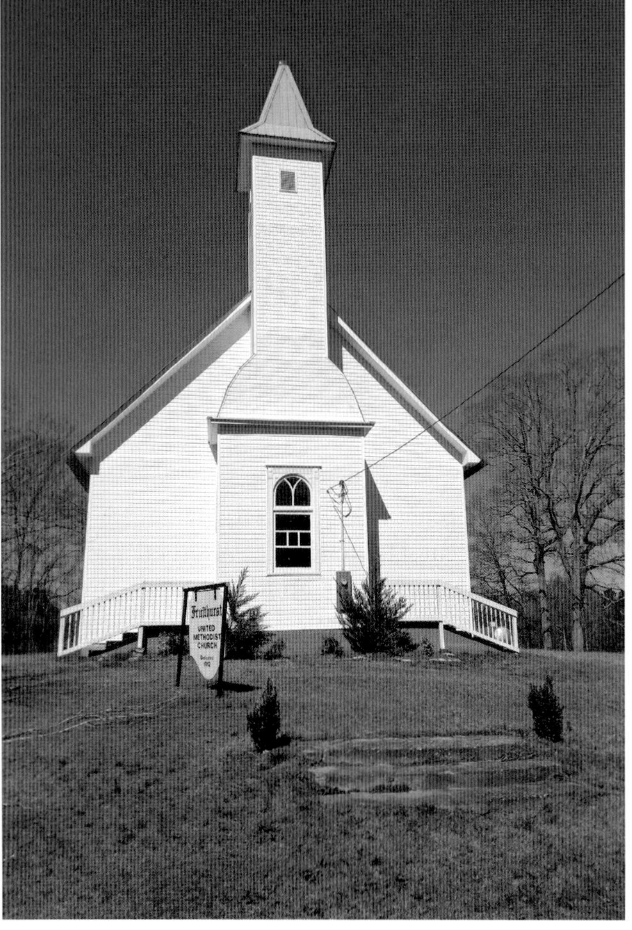

Above: Fruithurst, Alabama. Home to Fruithurst Winery, operated in the 1800s by Swedes, Danes and Norwegians who planted vineyards. A winery is now operating in the same location. *Wikipedia.*

Left: Fruithurst United Methodist Church, built in 1912, is a beautiful church in Fruithurst, a town once known for fine wines. *Personal collection.*

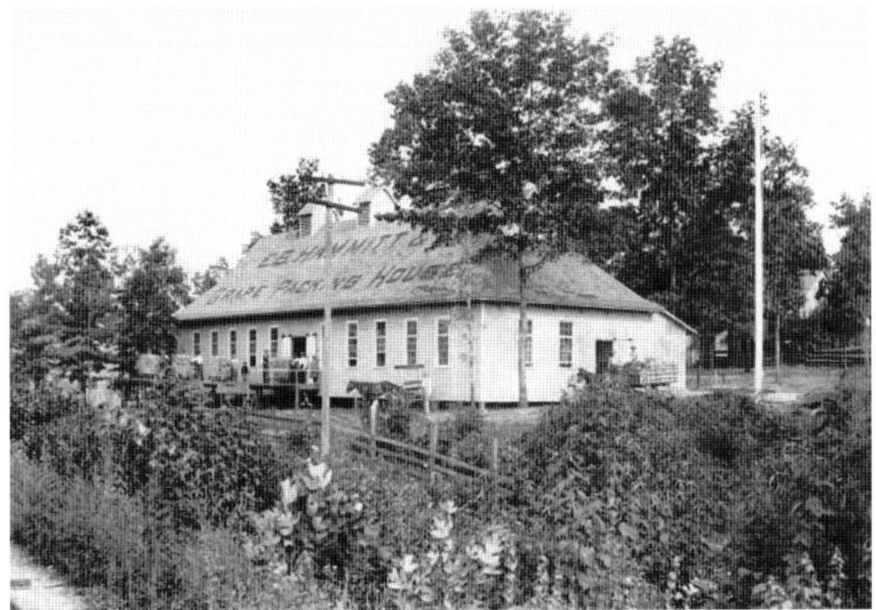

The E.B. Hammitt and Company grape-packing building in Fruithurst, Cleburne County. *Encyclopedia of Alabama*.

By 1898, more than three thousand acres of grapevines were under cultivation, and Fruithurst was producing twenty-three thousand gallons of various types of good-quality wine. Despite the recognition the Fruithurst wines received, outside circumstances took their toll on the town and the wine industry. In Alabama at that time, each county voted whether alcoholic beverages could be sold. Cleburne County voted dry, making it necessary to sell the Fruithurst wine to customers at greater distances, where the market was more competitive. Wine shipments were often damaged, causing further loss of business. The Great Depression diminished purchasing ability, creating a severely limited market for Fruithurst wine. Businesses and homes went up for sale, with many people abandoning their homes and traveling where they could get work. Elaborate structures were sold at sacrificial prices, "such as the Fruithurst Inn [which] was purchased by J.C. Bass of Carrollton, Georgia, and moved to Borden Springs in north Cleburne County (an area known for mineral springs) with hopes of turning it into a tourist resort."[92]

A ghost town now, Fruithurst can still boast of being a vineyard village with a winery business, operated by two hometown cousins, Josh and Dylan Laminack.

Borden-Wheeler Hotel

When the Fruithurst company went bankrupt, the Borden-Wheeler Company purchased the Fruithurst Inn, which was converted into a clubhouse where prospective buyers and investors could lodge. After the company purchased the clubhouse in 1903, it employed J.C. Bass of Carrollton to dismantle the building and move it the sixteen-mile distance to Borden Springs. Bass used mules and wagons to haul the lumber and used it to build the Borden-Wheeler Hotel. Borden Springs was in Calhoun County until 1866, when Calhoun and two other counties were divided to form Cleburne County. The Borden springs were discovered by John Borden in the 1890s. Bass developed a resort town for people who visited the mineral springs for therapeutic reasons. The resort quickly grew to have recreational and social features as well. Mrs. Stonewall Jackson and her grandchildren were among the socially prominent people who visited from Alabama and Georgia. "The hotel had 125 rooms, 9 concert pianos, running hot and cold water, electricity, a large outdoor swimming pool, a dance pavilion, and a golf course. Numerous chefs prepared the guest meals."[93]

> *The resort remained in business for thirty years under the ownership of three different owners. Due to increasing expenses and upkeep, the inn was closed in 1933 and it burned in 1934. All the things that were there at the beginning were untouched; the spring, the trees, and the mountains which were provided by nature. Borden Wheeler Hotel had the appearance of an important spa, comparable to the finest in the South, but it was too far elaborate for its location.*[94]

Chapter 5

DROWNED TOWNS

In the early 1900s, the small amount of electricity needed for streetlights, streetcars and residential lighting was generated from coal-fired dynamos. Cities required little electricity.[95] Change began on December 4, 1906, when William Patrick Lay incorporated the Alabama Power Company. Lay Dam in Coosa and Chilton Counties was the first hydroelectric plant built by Alabama Power. Other dams soon followed, each bearing the name of the entrepreneur whose vision drove construction in Central Alabama.[96]

An occasional article in a lake magazine or newspaper tells a story about workers' villages built near the construction site. The articles are interesting local history, but drowned towns were not as rare as they might seem. Where a dam was under construction, workers needed to live near the project for convenience. The story of each village is an interesting, integral part of the dam's history, and where possible, the town's story is told best by someone who lived in the village.

Cherokee Bluffs

The following narrative comes from Barbara Cole, whose father, Luther Ellison, worked in construction of Cherokee Bluffs' reservoir and machinery. In an interview in March 2019 at the Tallapoosa County Historical Museum in Dadeville, Barbara said, "My father was a level-three worker. He could do

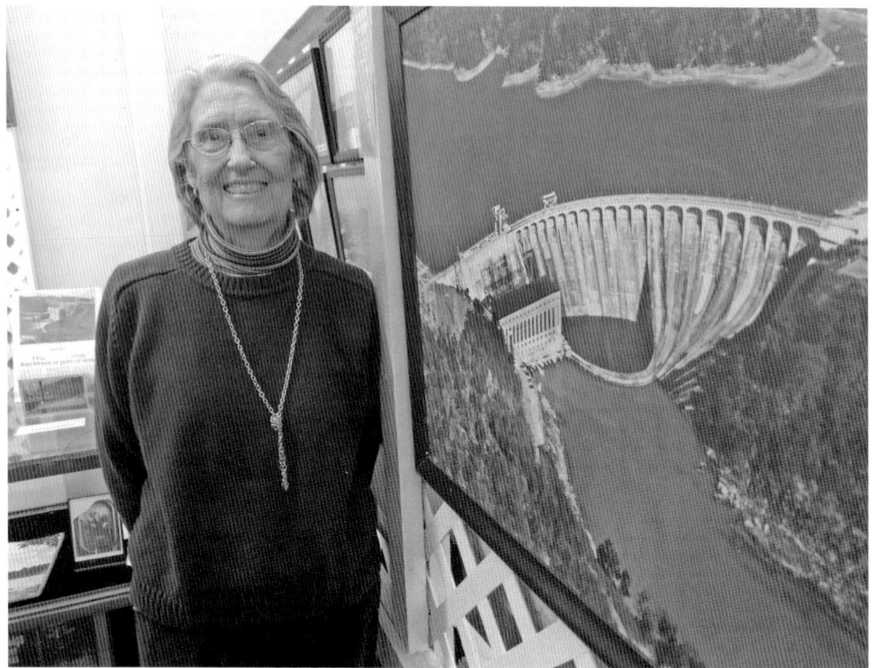

Barbara Cole stands by a picture of Martin Dam. She grew up in the Cherokee Bluffs village. *Personal collection.*

anything they asked him to do from keeping books to working on equipment and construction." Workers like Barbara's dad, superintendents, merchants, medical people and others were essential to creating the great dams that generated electricity for homes and businesses in Central Alabama.

In 1916, Alabama Power began purchasing lands that would be flooded when the waters were released from Martin Dam. At the time, Thomas Wesley Martin was president of the Alabama Power Company. Later, the dam and the lake were named in honor of him.

Cherokee Bluff Village was built in the 1920s. Workers and their families lived there while Martin Dam was under construction. Barbara Ellison Cole remembers growing up in the village, where she lived with her mother, Claire, and her father, Luther Ellison. The town had stores, churches, a school and a hospital, where, during World War II, wounded soldiers were sent to be treated and to recover. Prisoners of war received the same treatment as the American boys. Fort McClellan sent soldiers to protect the dam. Sea planes were in and out frequently during World War II.

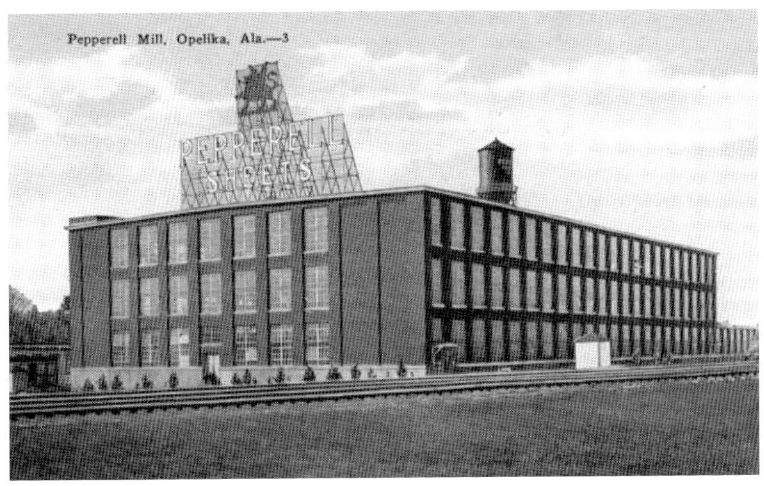

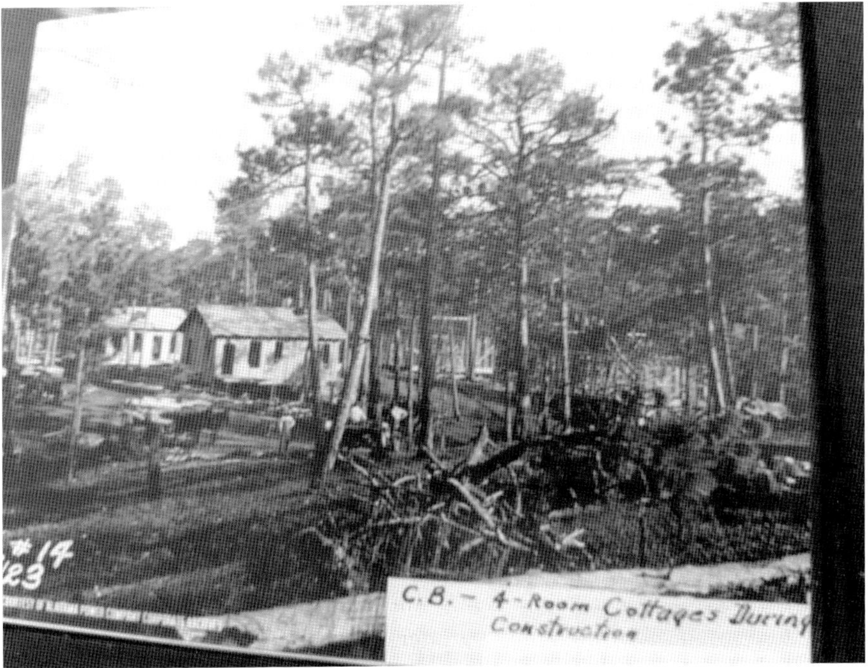

Top: Pepperell sheet plant in Opelika, Alabama, pictured in its years of operation. A baseball and athletic field was built in the village in 1930. *Robert Noles*/Opelika Observer.

Bottom: Four-room cottages with large yards for workers and their families under construction at Cherokee Bluffs. Palomino pony rides are being offered for children. *Tallapoosa Historical Association Museum.*

> *My favorite thing to do when I was a kid was to go to the plant and ride the elevator. The elevator went all the way to the top of the plant, all the way under water. It was a beautiful elevator. It was lined with copper and the gate was brass. I would go to that plant and ride the elevator up and down, up and down, and more up and down. The superintendent said to me one day, "Now Barbara, you can ride the elevator, but you can't do it but twice a day." My brother's favorite thing was fishing below the dam. There was a huge rock....He would swim out and fish from that rock. At that time, they did not blow the horn when they let the water through, and he got caught on that rock. He had to sit on the edge for hours until the water was no longer released from the dam. Water was moving so fast you couldn't get out to the rock nor back to the shore. So, this ended my brother's fishing out on the rock.*[97]

Martin Dam was completed in 1926; the lake was filled on April 23, 1928. At the time Martin Dam was opened, floodwaters released into Lake Martin traveled over thirty miles up the Tallapoosa River. Lake Martin was the largest man-made body of water in the world. The 168-foot-high dam stretched two thousand feet across the Tallapoosa River gorge at Cherokee Bluffs.

The dedication ceremony was attended by prominent Alabama Power officials and local businessmen and was well documented and featured in numerous magazines and newspapers. Russell Crossroads has a large display of lake pictures, the dam in progress and the workers' village.

Cherokee Bluffs had cows, horses, farm animals and barns. Alabama Power provided garden spots for residents of the village. The plans were that the village houses and buildings like the stores, school and hospital would be torn down, and families would be relocated. The village also had a cemetery where beloved family members were buried. The graves had to be dug up and corpses taken to the communities where their families planned to live, such as Alexander City and more distant rural communities. More than nine hundred graves were disinterred and moved before water was released from the dam. Wagons used to transport coffins were constructed of wood in the basement of the Duncan store in Alexander City. The coffins stayed in the basement until they were needed. Care was taken to avoid a mix-up between new and used caskets, and possibly more than one occupied coffin was discovered and gave a fright to the person who raised the lid and saw a corpse. People were given the opportunity to stop by and identify the man, but efforts were unsuccessful. No one claimed the body, so the community

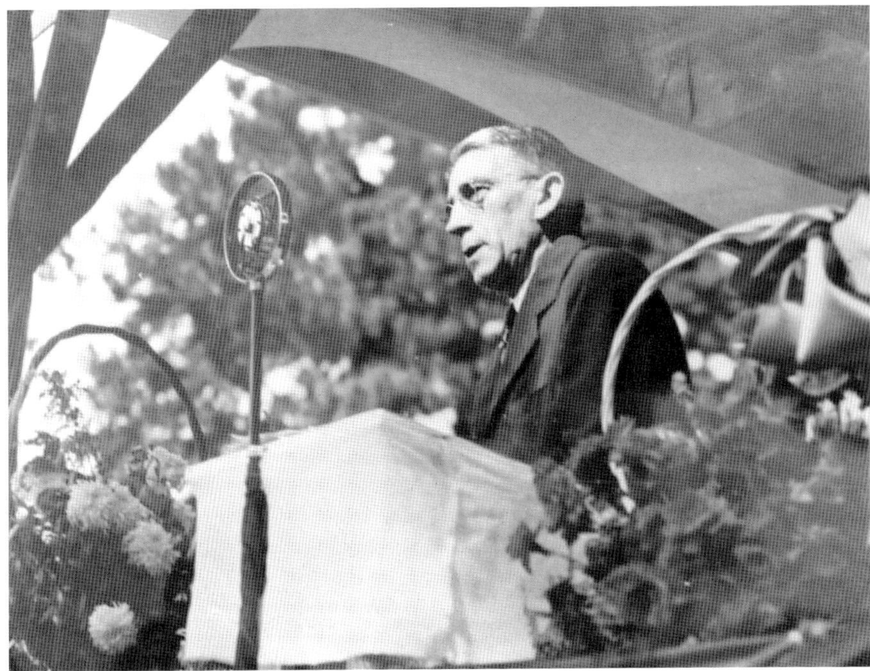

In 1926, Martin Dam was named for Alabama Power president Thomas Wesley Martin. In 1936, the dam was officially dedicated by Benjamin Russell. *Encyclopedia of Alabama.*

buried him in the old cemetery at the edge of town. One of the Duncan wagons used to transport coffins from Cherokee Bluffs can be seen in the Tallapoosa County Museum in Dadeville. The museum would be a divine place for ghosts to live and surprise the visitors, but no unusual experiences have been reported.

According to local lore, not everything was removed from the village before the dam waters were released. A church with a bell still inside the steeple was left behind. When the current moved the water and swayed the bell, you could hear it ring, reminding people of the community that once surrounded the old church.

The second tale requires more imagination to believe. The story goes that an old man who raised coon dogs was bought out when the lake was built, as were his neighbors. Every time one of the dogs died, the old man buried it behind his house. He planned to move the dogs' graves to a place where they would not be submerged in the lake water. But his health failed, and he was not able to move them before he passed. He had pleaded with his

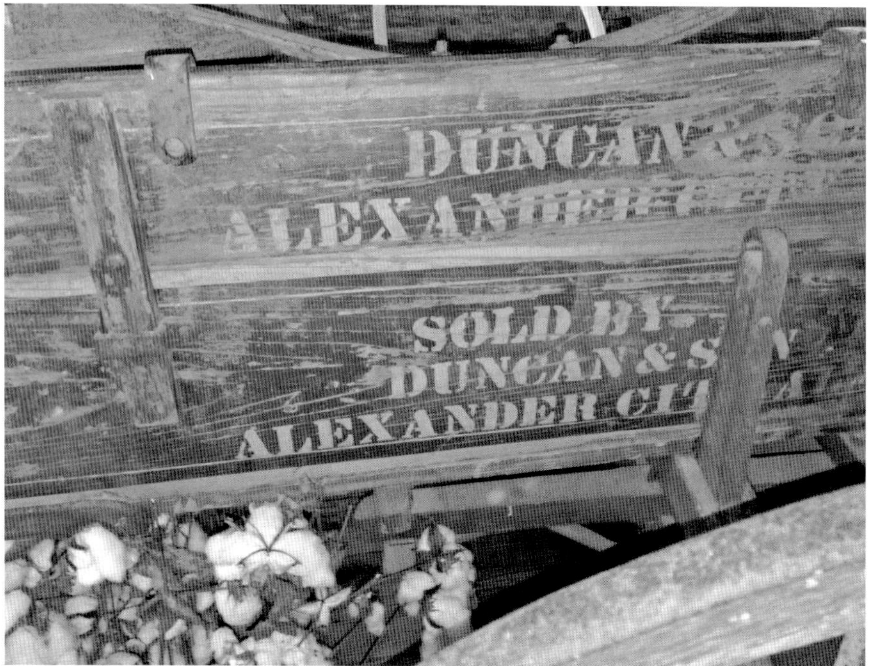

On display at the Dadeville Museum is one of the Duncan wagons used to transport the coffins from the Cherokee Bluffs cemetery. *Tallapoosa Historical Association Museum.*

wife to move the dogs before the water was released from the dam. Despite her promise, the wife did not move the dogs, and the crates and remains of the dogs were submerged when the dam waters were released. Knowing the story, some people claim that on a clear day, the sound of the coon dogs baying and chasing a phantom prey disturbs the silence of the sunken city and their old hunting fields.

Cherokee Bluffs was one of the largest towns submerged under the surging waters of Martin Dam. The communities of Susanna (Susanna) and Benson, including several houses and churches, were razed, and the company relocated twelve cemeteries containing 923 graves. At its peak, Susanna had a gold mine and post office, a school, a church and several mills, such as a shingle mill, a gristmill, a sawmill and a blacksmith shop.[98]

MORE ALABAMA DAMS

Weiss Dam

The Weiss Dam was named after Fernand C. Weiss, a chief engineer of Alabama Power. The first dam built by Alabama Power construction program, Weiss Dam was located near Leesburg in Cherokee County. The remains of the workers' village and Lawrence Cemetery were submerged beneath Weiss Lake. When the water level is at its lowest, part of the cemetery is visible. Most of Weiss Lake is in Cherokee County, which borders Etowah County north of Gadsden in the company's Eastern Division. Construction on the dam started on July 13, 1958, and Weiss began generating power on June 5, 1961. The three generators had a generating capacity of 87,750 kilowatts. Second only to Alabama Power's Lake Martin, the reservoir is 52 miles long and has 447 miles of shoreline. The dam water release further developed the Coosa River in the late 1950s and the 1960s.

Weiss Lake is known as the "Crappie Capital of the World" and a popular place to fish for other species like largemouth bass, spotted bass,

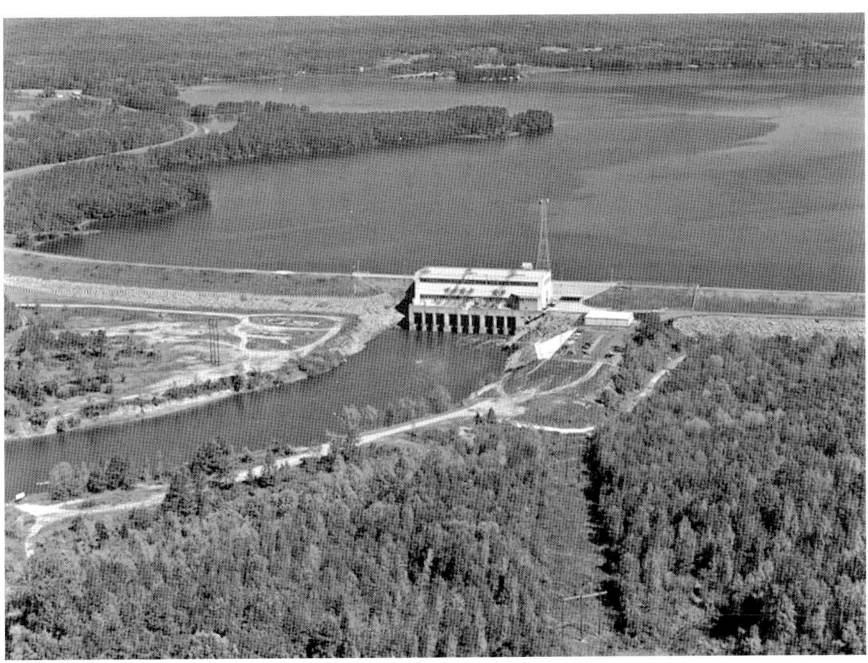

Weiss Dam. *Courtesy of Alabama Power, Encyclopedia of Alabama.*

white bass, striped bass, hybrid striper, bluegill, longear sunfish, redear sunfish, channel catfish, blue catfish, flathead catfish and freshwater drum. It is part of the Alabama Scenic River Trail. Other activities include jet skiing, sailing and swimming.

Wheeler Dam

Wheeler was the second dam Tennessee Valley Association built, beginning in 1933 and finishing in 1936 at a cost of $87,655,000. Located at Town Creek, the structure is 72 feet high, stretching over 6,342 feet across the Tennessee River. The reservoir extends over 1,027 miles of shoreline and 67,070 acres of water surface. The hydroelectric facility has a storage capacity of 326,500 acre-feet. Before the project began, TVA had to clear 12,638 of the 31,228 acres. The construction provided economic relief to thousands of people. TVA, at peak production, employed 4,700 people. Structures were removed and relocated, including 840 families and 176 graves.

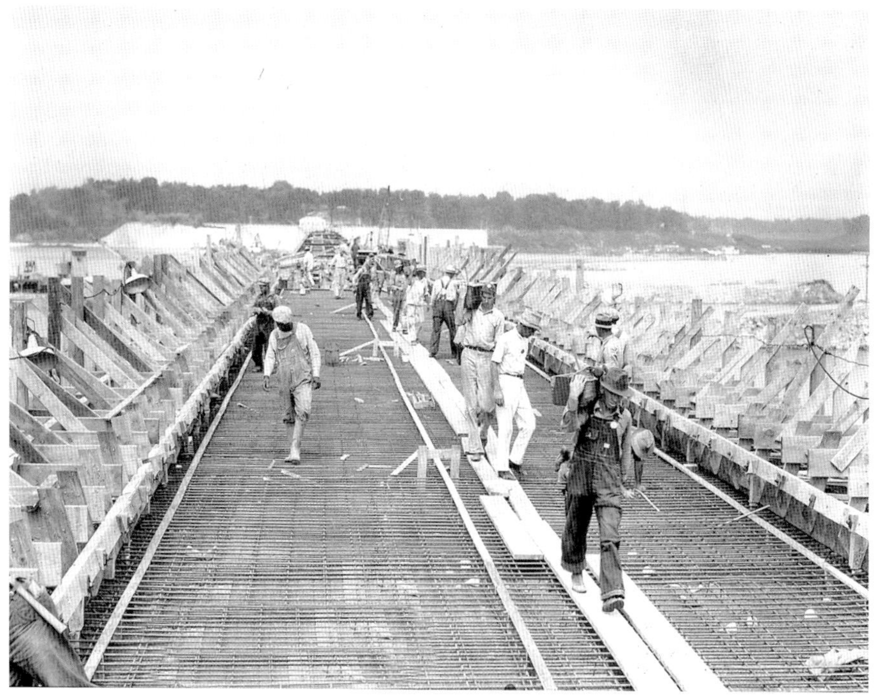

Wheeler Dam, named for General Joseph Wheeler, was the first project started by the TVA in 1933 and was completed in 1936. *Tennessee River Valley, "TVA Wheeler Dam and Reservoir."*

Wheeler Dam is named for U.S. Congressman Joseph Wheeler. The dam was placed in the National Register of Historic Places in 2016. "Today, Wheeler Reservoir is a major recreation and tourist center. Along with camping, boating and fishing, visitors enjoy the Wheeler National Wildlife Refuge, located several miles upstream from the dam. The refuge features Alabama's only significant concentration of wintering Canada geese."[99]

Logan Martin Lake, "Lake of a Thousand Coves"

When Logan Martin Lake dam waters were released in 1963, it took towns and private lakes with it. The benefits of the dams in Central Alabama were enormous, but the dams also caused the extinction of thirty-six species. According to the Center for Biological Diversity, the loss created the greatest extinction in modern North American history. Prior to the release of water, construction workers were given permission to remove parts of the houses. The windows, doors and other materials were transported in mule-drawn wagons for use in building new homes or repairing old. Sometimes an entire structure was saved for a community purpose. Two small private lakes,

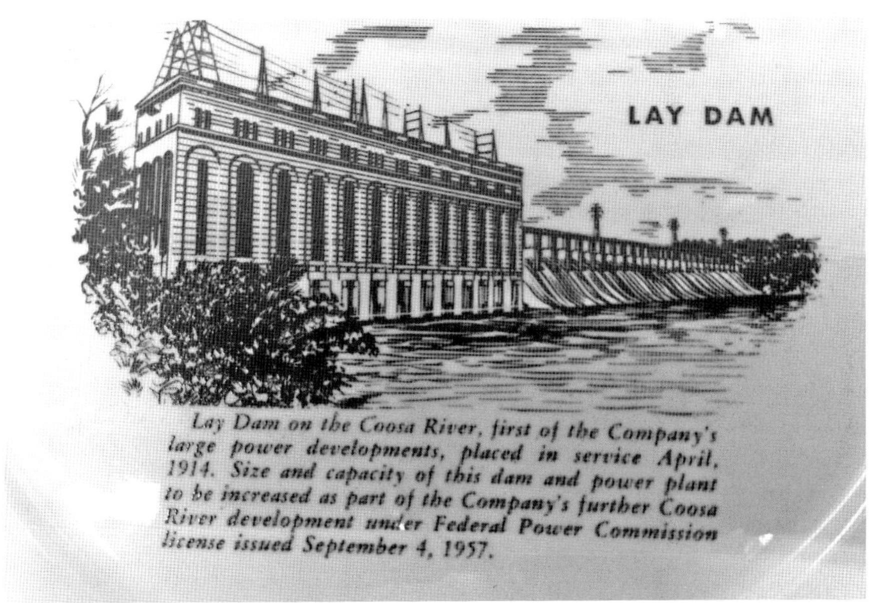

Lay Dam on the Coosa River, April 1914. The first of the plants put into service by Alabama Power. *Tallapoosa Historical Association Museum.*

Avondale and Harmon Lakes, were destroyed as well. Avondale Lake, known originally as Waites Lake, was created from a cluster of ice-cold lakes in an area known as River Oaks and Harmon Island. Waites Lake was built by the Waites family in the early 1900s next to the old route of U.S. Highway 231.

> *In the 1940s, the lake property was bought by the mill as a pure water source for its plant in Pell City and also to provide free outdoor recreation for everyone connected with Avondale, which included the majority of Pell City folks as well as lots of Sylacaugans. Conversely, Harmon Lake…was open to the general public, but the owners charged for everything.*[100]

Numerous homes and communities and surrounding schools and churches were covered when the dam waters were released. Thousands of acres were covered, and all or a part of towns like Benson were partially covered.

Benson, Alabama

Named for its founder, former slave John Benson, the town of Benson was in Elmore and Tallapoosa Counties. Benson's story takes him from laboring in the cotton fields of the plantation owner James Benson to being the founder of the all-Black town that bore his name.

John Jackson Benson

In the 1800s, Virginia plantation owner James Benson owned thousands of acres near Kowaliga during a time when growing cotton was a thriving business. The industry's success depended on slave labor. Benson died in 1863, and neighbors purchased sections of the Benson farmland. John Benson was born in 1850 on the Benson plantation, where he labored until the Civil War ended and slaves were emancipated. After the Civil War and the emancipation of slaves, John worked in the Cahaba coal mine in Shelby County from 1870 to 1880. His son William was born in 1873. With the dream of returning to the Kowaliga Creek area, John saved as much as he could of the $10 he earned each month. When he had saved $100, he moved his family back to Kowaliga. He was able to obtain credit and purchase 160 acres of the old Benson plantation land. John built a nice home for his wife, Lucy Jane Wiley, and their children, William and three daughters: Laura Emma Benson, Lula M. Benson and Martha "Mattie" Benson. He became a successful farmer. With good business skills, he earned enough money to buy more acreage. Using his personal financial resources, he was able to underwrite mortgages for other farmers in Tallapoosa and Elmore Counties.

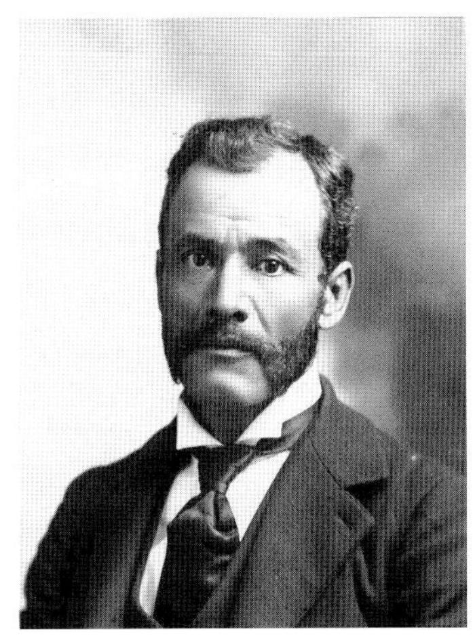

John Benson was a successful farmer with a wife, son and three daughters: Laura Emma Benson, Lula M. Benson and Martha "Mattie" Benson. *Russell Lands.*

If John's story ended here, it would be a remarkable testament to how a former slave persevered through slavery and labored in coal mines to purchase a part of the farm where he worked as a slave. As admirable as this achievement was, John's vision went much further. Part of his plan was to build an all-Black community with nice homes and businesses. His biggest plan was to build a school to educate former slaves and their families and teach them skills to support themselves and build the town of Benson. Determined to provide his son with an education he did not have the opportunity to acquire, he sent William to Washington, D.C., where he attended and graduated from Howard University. When William returned to Benson, he, John and other community members worked to establish the Kowaliga Industrial School. The first building was paid for with contributions from seventy Black men in the Benson community. A large part of the school was supported by the Friends of Negro Education and eastern philanthropic organizations.[101]

Many Benson supporters were the same philanthropic organizations that contributed to Booker T. Washington's school at Tuskegee, established on July 4, 1881. The purpose of the Kowaliga Industrial School was primarily to teach skills to former slaves surrounding Benson. Tuskegee Institute operated "under a charter from the Alabama legislature for the purpose of training teachers in Alabama. Tuskegee's program provided students with both academic and vocational training."[102]

John, through hard work, perseverance and God-given abilities, moved from the humble status of a slave to establishing the town of Benson, named in his honor. The astounding achievements of John and his son William were so great in the late 1800s and early 1900s that to this day, the older generation of people in the Alexander City area remember what they

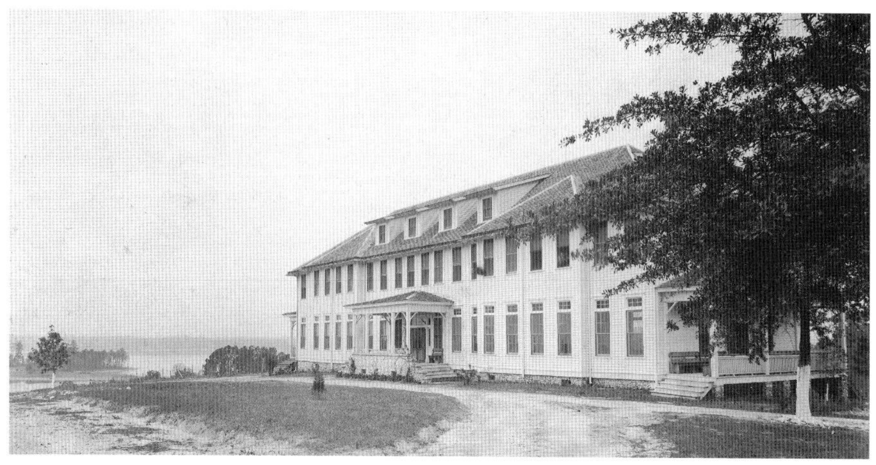

Kowaliga Academic and Industrial Institute, Patron's Hall, 1910. Students learned domestic skills and occupational training. Kowaliga Creek is in the background. *Russell Lands.*

were able to achieve in the Kowaliga area. They marveled at the Bensons' ingenuity, sacrifice and philanthropic work to better the lives of hundreds of children and families who lived in or near Benson.

In the early 1900s, after the Reconstruction period, there were northern investors who contributed to the work of Black businessmen and educators to help them sustain and expand their enterprises to lessen the handicap of spending most of their lives in a state of slavery. John's first dream was to purchase the land where he had worked as a slave and then to cultivate the fields and establish the town of Benson. Most important to John Benson, he wanted to provide his son William with the education he and other slaves were unable to obtain. He was successful in achieving all of those goals.

William developed the same work ethics that John displayed throughout his life, first as a slave and then as a free man. William was dedicated to establishing the Kowaliga Industrial School and the Dixie Railroad line. But it was John's vision of helping other former slaves to gain an education that built and sustained the all-Black town of Benson. Through the Kowaliga Industrial School, they gained academic and occupational training. They constructed comfortable homes for their families, community organizations, a profitable sawmill and turpentine business. In 1898, the town of Benson was incorporated.

In 1892, William began his studies at Howard College in Washington, D.C., and graduated in 1895. As a well-educated Black man during the Reconstruction days, he could have remained in the North and chosen

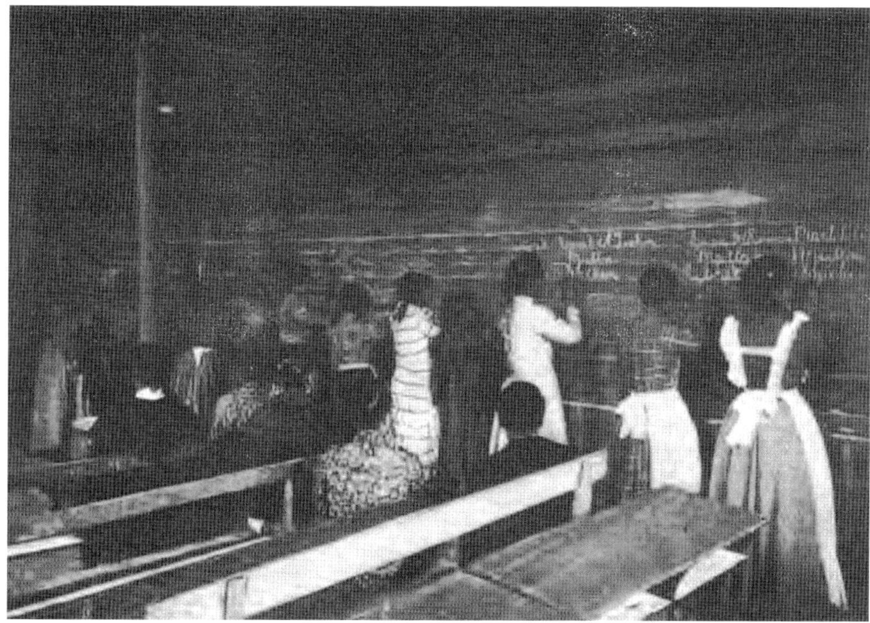

Students at the chalkboard are learning skills to take care of themselves and contribute to betterment of the community. *Russell Lands.*

a profession that would bring him prominence and wealth. But, like his father, William returned to Kowaliga to help the Black people in the community. He was concerned for his people as violence erupted in Kowaliga and surrounding areas. At least eight Black men and women were lynched in Alabama, and an undetermined number of Blacks were visited by night riders who threatened and severely beat members of the Black sharecroppers' union. Like his father, William knew that his people could only escape their circumstances through education. Over a two-year period, working between crops, William, John and neighbors completed the two-story schoolhouse. William traveled Tallapoosa and Elmore Counties soliciting financial support for the school. Local Black families, investors from nearby Alexander City and northern benefactors contributed money for the cause.

William expanded his solicitations to include the same northern financiers who contributed generously to Tuskegee Institute, less than thirty miles away. William and Booker T. Washington, the founder of the Tuskegee Institute, had similar goals of educating the Black people in Central Alabama. Washington sat on the board of the Kowaliga school and advised William on how to solicit funds for the school and operate Kowaliga Industrial School. Washington was committed to attracting students and focusing on higher levels of education, training them to be teachers. With this goal in mind, Tuskegee attracted students from a greater distance than the Kowaliga Industrial School. The school focused on both academic instruction and teaching domestic and industrial skills to the local children and those in surrounding communities. By 1913, the school had enrolled 320 students who lived within walking distance. The school employed 12 teachers who engaged the students in a broad range of activities, such as music, church and rhetorical events. The students were expected to perform work of some kind to contribute to the school's operation. Girls worked in the mess hall and cleaned the dormitories. In addition to their academic studies, the boys applied the skills of carpentry, handiwork and operation of the turpentine mill.

William Benson learned a great deal about establishing a school from Booker T. Washington, who at age twenty-five was principal of Tuskegee Normal School for Colored Teachers. Benson and community members built the Kowaliga Academic and Industrial School, as Washington and his students had built the Tuskegee school. When Washington came to Tuskegee, there were no buildings in which to hold classes. On July 4, 1881, Washington taught students in the African Methodist Episcopal Zion Church. Like in Benson, instructors and students were African American. Instructors designed the school, and the students constructed it. Four years later, in 1885, the first students graduated from Tuskegee.

Will Benson started Kowaliga Academic and Industrial Institute in 1895. It was incorporated in 1897. The following were members of the board of trustees:

Clarence H. Kelly, New York, New York
D.N. Barney, Hartford, Connecticut
Miss Alice Lewisohn, New York
Miss Emily Howland, Sherwood, New York
Oswald Garrison Villard, New York, New York
Reverend Floyd W. Tompkins, Philadelphia, Pennsylvania
Mrs. Isabel C. Barrows, Croton-on-Hudson, New York
Jackson Robinson, Kowaliga, Alabama
John J. Benson, Kowaliga, Alabama
Alexander Meadows, Benson, Alabama
William E. Benson, secretary and treasurer, Benson, Alabama

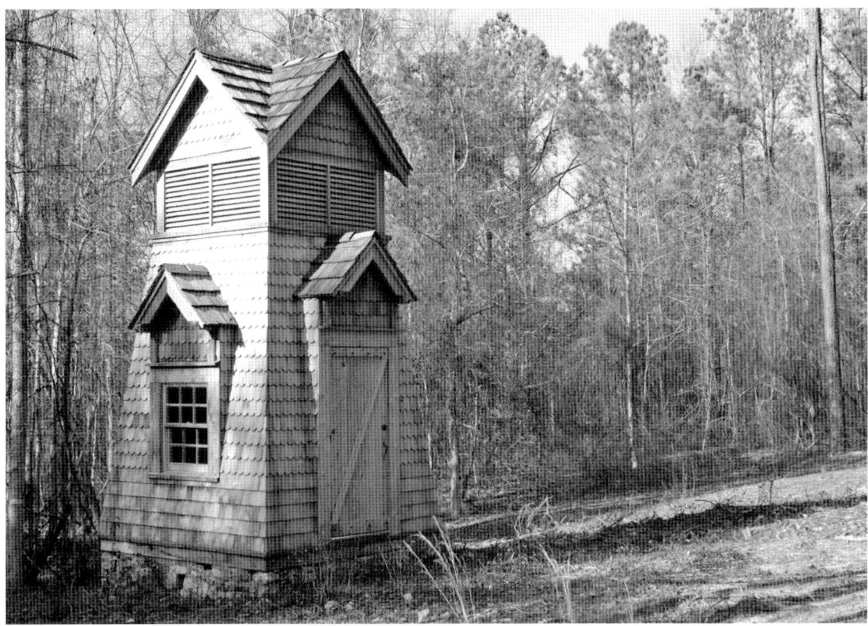

The ringing of the watch tower bell called children to the Kowaliga Academic and Industrial Institute from outside Benson. *Russell Lands.*

For over thirty years, the children of Benson and a few other communities in Elmore and Tallapoosa County were educated at the Kowaliga school. In 1895, William Benson established the Dixie Industrial Company, which sponsored the Kowaliga school. He returned north and gained the support of Villard, chairman of the board, who influenced English and Canadian firms to contribute to the building of the railroad for the transporting of timber and turpentine products to larger markets. Benson employed hundreds of community members to operate a sawmill and turpentine plant. They were able to use local resources to build a railroad to Alexander City and ship their products to national and international markets.

The completion of the Dixie line made it possible to sell large quantities of turpentine, lumber and cotton in the South and overseas to Germany and other countries. The years between 1913 and 1916 brought prosperity to the Dixie Industrial Company and the town of Benson. The onset of World War I in 1916 changed everything. The mill products could not be shipped overseas. The price of cotton dropped from around fifteen cents a pound to three or four cents a pound, affecting the market at home and abroad. A three-month shutdown of the railroad, sawmills and turpentine

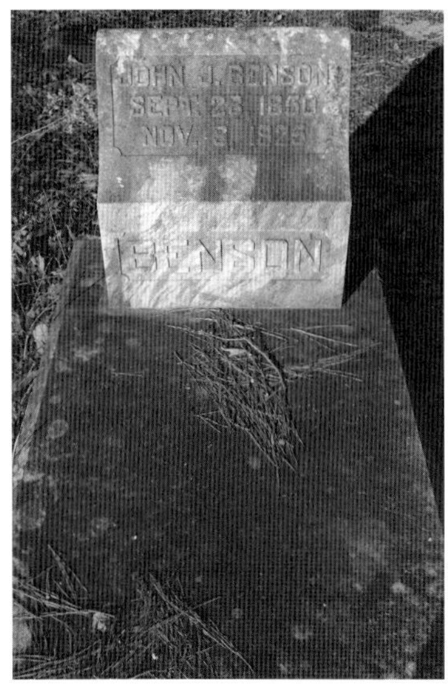

John Jackson Benson's headstone. Benson was a former slave and the founder of the all-Black town of Benson, which was incorporated in 1898. *Russell Lands.*

stills forced the company into bankruptcy. Many people left Benson to search for jobs elsewhere.

Local people purchased the railroad and bought the land, and several companies cut and hauled the timber. Some of these companies were Watts and Levy, Russell and Steverson, Walter Crow, Towns Brothers, W.L. Stowe and J.R. Black.[103] John Jackson Benson died on November 8, 1925, after establishing a large farm, a town with businesses, churches and the Kowaliga Industrial School that lifted former slaves and their families from a life devoid of opportunities into being a part of an independent all-Black town.

After the death of William Benson on October 10, 1915, the school operated until the waters of Lake Martin prevented children from Elmore County from being able to reach it in 1926. The school was sold, and the main building was converted into a hotel years later. People from Alexander City and other nearby towns traveled to the hotel and enjoyed luxurious meals and orchestras from Birmingham, like the earlier mineral spring resorts in Talladega County had provided. A small building was constructed for the remaining students and operated until it was consolidated with the Alexander City School System in September 1966. As a board member of Kowaliga Industrial School, Booker T. Washington visited the school and advised William on its operation. The young Ben Russell of Russell Lands recalled, in a 2016 interview with this author, that Washington and Ben sat on the front porch of the Russells' modest home and discussed the progress of Benson and Tuskegee schools and other timely topics. The following narrative is quoted from the autobiographical "Pre–Ben Russell History."

> *A most interesting aspect of the pre–Ben Russell history is that of Will Benson, who owned much of the land in the Kowaliga Creek area of the present Lake Martin. Mr. William (Will) E. Benson, a local black graduate of Howard University in Washington, DC…founded the*

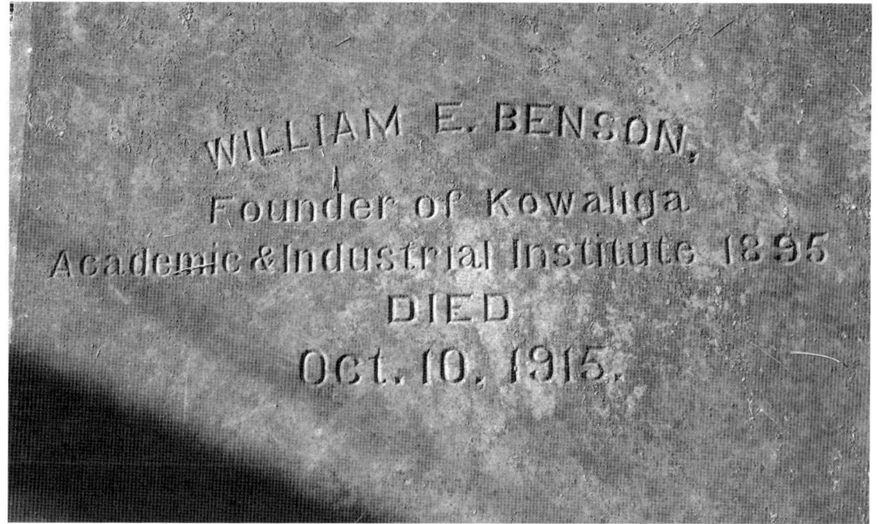

William Benson's gravestone. Will Benson (1873–1915) started the Kowaliga Academic and Industrial Institute in 1895. It was incorporated in 1897. *Russell Lands.*

Kowaliga School in 1895 to improve the lives of the local black population. In 1897 the name was changed to The Kowaliga Academic and Industrial Institute. Unfortunately, however, WWI curtailed the overseas sale of one of the principal products of the Benson timberland, turpentine. In the mid-1920s the Institute's landholdings were separated by the rising waters behind the newly completed Martin Dam. Cotton prices also dropped to 5 cents per pound about that time. These and other unfortunate situations eventually forced the Benson enterprises and the school to close. It was absorbed, to a degree, by nearby Tuskegee Institute. Many people moved from the area of Lake Martin in those days, fearing malaria and other diseases, which had been publicized during the earlier building of the Panama Canal. Dr. Gargus had by then discovered the cause and cure for malaria and was on hand to ensure the eradication of the infamous mosquito, during the building of the Panama Canal.

Mr. Ben later purchased the Benson Sawmill, the Kowaliga School and some of its property. The school's farmland was then included in the farming activities of Dixie Farms. He employed many of its personnel in an attempt to convert the school's central facility into a large hotel. He also included many of the school's black families in his innovative family-farming program on the Russell lands. This was another first step on the road to real independence for some of these families.[104]

Chapter 6

TURPENTINE MILLS

From the late nineteenth century through World War I, the South was the nation's leading lumber producer, peaking in 1901, when southern producers supplied one-third of the nation's lumber.[105]

During the years of the Great Depression from 1929 until 1947, more than fifteen million Americans were unemployed nationwide. In cities, there were charity bread lines. Men carried signs pleading for work. In rural communities, there were even fewer jobs, among them farming, sharecropping and sawmilling. But the demand for lumber kept the small sawmills busy. Wood was needed to build houses and to fill military orders. Thus, jobs were available for those who did not mind dangerous work. In Coosa County, there were many small peckerwood sawmills. As the timber thinned in one forest, they moved to another, so work could be temporary. However, some jobs were more stable. In 1931, Isaac Richard Anderson established the Ralph Lumber Company in western Coosa County. He employed over two hundred men and built a sawmill village that grew to a population of five or six hundred people. Men were glad to find work and a place for their family to live.

At the time, the mill produced about twenty-five to thirty thousand board feet per day. Oxen were used to snake the logs to the small steam mill. John Davidson was ten years old when his family arrived in the sawmill camp; later as an adult, he recorded the story of the lumber company and the Hillwood sawmill village in the book *The Hillwood Story*. The information in this article is paraphrased and summarized from Davidson's book, beginning with a summary of how he and his family learned about Hillwood. The owner, Isaac Richard Anderson, was called "Mr. Rich" by the workers. Davidson described him as a kind person who cared about his workers and their families. He and two of his sons, Ralph and Johnnie, stayed in the village boardinghouse. Anderson's wife, Ollie; their two daughters, Edith and Nona; and Isaac, the third son, remained in Laurel, Mississippi, to take care of Mr. Rich's other businesses, a Ford dealership and another sawmill. The village was surrounded by forty-five thousand acres of long-leaf pine and hardwood.

Davidson recalled the difficult circumstances that brought his family to Hillwood. His father had been unemployed for a year when his brother Ben sent a letter informing him that a new lumber camp in Coosa County was hiring. The family loaded up their belongings and headed there. John's father was hired as a sawyer, someone who cut wood with a crosscut saw. John attended Hillwood School and Church, both held in the same building. He and other village boys performed daily chores of carrying water from a spring or well to meet the family's need for water and brought in wood for the potbelly heater and wood-burning stove. He did his homework by a kerosene lamp, as there was no electricity for the houses.

The sawmill business and the town of Hillwood thrived from 1931 to 1947—during the hard years of the Great Depression (1929–36) and World War II (1939–45). The village consisted of approximately five or six hundred people who welcomed the opportunity to work and to have a church and medical help on site. Cutting timber and sawing logs on the hilly terrain was dangerous and could easily result in an accident. The village was self-sustaining. Residents raised cattle, hogs and other animals to be slaughtered for meat. Mr. Rich brought several herds of cattle and let them graze in the woods. He fed them hay through the winter. He built a cattle gap across the road to keep them on company land. The village was much like an old western ranch. There were saddle horses. Archie Pearce, a log truck driver, and a man nicknamed Cowboy would round up the cattle. Then several men would hold the cows down while one applied the branding iron. When the cattle were slaughtered, Mr. Jim Camp was the chief butcher. When the job was finished, Mr. Rich sold some of the beef in Hillwood. The butcher cut a quarter beef into round steaks that cost twenty cents per pound. Davidson recalled, "I never knew there was any other cut of beef until I went into the army."

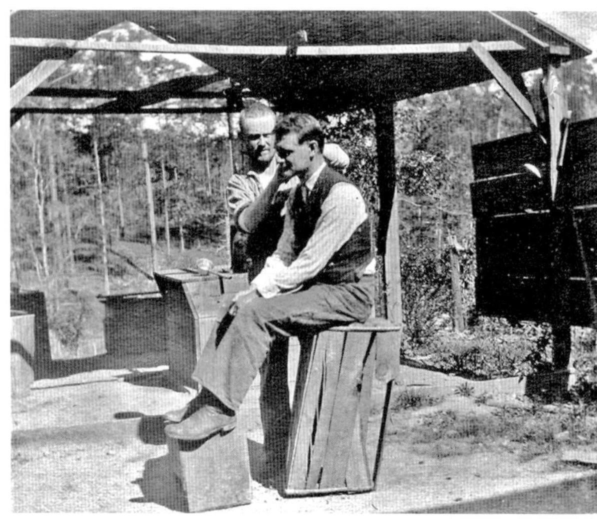

A sawmill worker gets a haircut while he sits on a large crate. Behind him is a dipper and a well. *Alabama Department of Archives and History.*

Mr. Rich bought truckloads of razorback hogs and turned them loose to roam the fields. Some took refuge in the woods and became wild. There were other hogs better suited to be slaughtered and used for bacon and ham. Mr. Rich also bought several herds of cattle and turned them loose to graze. There was only one road to enter or leave the property. Other animals included two pet monkeys. They were kept in a large cage for a couple of years in front of the boardinghouse, where they entertained the boarders with their antics. Then they were released into the woods.

Most of the houses were built in a shotgun style with no porches and no screen windows. Workers made the mistake of using green lumber to build the houses. After the sun dried the boards, they shrank, leaving large gaps in the boards. The workers used one-by-four batten boards to cover the cracks. The houses had no electricity for appliances of any kind—no lights, no running water, no toilets. Wood-burning potbelly stoves heated the houses. A wood-burning cook stove heated iron skillets for frying pork or beef and boiling vegetables. The food was kept warm with the heat from a four-gallon reservoir. There was ample wood, split logs, pine knots and pine scraps used for fuel, cooking food and heating the house.

Boys in each family kept their families supplied with wood and carried water for cooking, bathing and washing clothes. If there were no sons, the family would pay thirty-five to fifty cents per week for a boy in the village to carry their water. The women washed clothes near a spring or well to have enough water handy. There was a boiling pot for washing work clothes and a rubbing board to loosen the dirt before washing them. Usually, a bench nearby had two or three tubs filled with clean water for rinsing the clothes. Clothes were boiled for twenty minutes or more in the first wash. There was a great deal of emptying tubs and pouring fresh water into them to rinse out the soap. The clothes would then be squeezed and wrung out as tightly as possible. The ladies shook out the wrinkles, using wooden clothespins to fasten them on a wire, wiped clean with a rag to keep rust from staining the freshly washed clothes. The ladies were rewarded at the end of the day with fresh-smelling clothes, towels and sheets ready to be folded and put away. Washdays were followed by ironing days. Ironing was an all-day job too. Flat irons were heated on the stove, on the hearth or outside in a fire built under a shade tree, where the women would set up a board to iron overalls, shirts and dresses.

Water was necessary for household tasks like washing dishes, which required two dishpans, one filled with soap and water and the other with hot rinsing water. After washing and rinsing plates and glasses, the women then dried them with a large cloth. When the table was cleared, the children did their homework while Dad read the newspaper or Bible under the light of two or three kerosene lamps. The Hillwood church served as both a place for worship and a place for school. Under the supervision of the two teachers, one group of students studied on one side of the church while the other group was taught so that students learned from both teachers. The winter months were especially uncomfortable. Students sat on church benches, and the room was heated by a small wood-burning heater.

In 1932, the children went from Hillwood to Mount Moriah School, about a mile away. Ben Davidson took the younger children in his old green Buick, and the older ones walked. Mount Moriah had more space and a larger wood heater. Teachers included Laura Mae Dickinson, who taught at Hillwood and later at Mount Moriah. Luke Rayfield was the principal and teacher. He was followed by Mr. Luker, Mr. Bryant and Mrs. Hanna. Other buildings included the main office, the shop garage and the doctor's office that was next to the post office building. Mrs. McMann was the first and only postmistress. The commissary was the only place where workers could use their company coins, called "jugaloos." Real money was called "main line." There were dry goods, meat, canned goods and a few truck and automobile parts for sale. Beside the commissary, a large warehouse stored dry goods and a large refrigerator to preserve meat and other perishable items.

In June 1946, Sterling Lumber and Supply Company purchased the Ralph Company and continued operations for over a year and then moved to Goodwater. It did not purchase the land or the timber. No structures remain where Hillwood Village was. Hillwood closed in 1946; only a few people can remember their parents or grandparents talking about Ralph Lumber Company and the little sawmill town where people lived and worked in the Depression years and through World War II.

In an interview, Mr. Carel Smith, at ninety years old, remembered Hillwood. "One day I skipped school and rode on one of those big lumber trucks to the holding pond at Hillwood and watched the men work. The work in this hilly area was extremely dangerous. There were bad, steep hills. There were many accidents, some where men were killed or injured." Smith said lots of lumber was used for military ships. "Hillwood had the best long-leaf pine timber in the world. Big, tall pines that had never been cut. They were rich with turpentine." He compared the village of Hillwood to Cutter Gap, the small mountain town Catherine Marshall wrote about in her book *Christy*. The property has returned to nature; trees have grown tall again, and few people could find the site of the sawmill village. But at one time, before the pulpwooding industry replaced the sawmill, people lived in self-sustaining camps in a setting of wildlife and uncut trees that seemed to touch the sky. The trees were cut and shipped to the military ships, lumberyards and construction companies. The industry provided necessary income to meet the families' needs in times when employment was difficult to find.[106]

Chapter 7

TEXTILE MILLS

Although Alexander City textile industries started in the late 1800s and early 1900s, cotton manufacturing in Tallapoosa County occurred much earlier, before statehood (1819) and before the county was formed (1832). In 1796, Benjamin Hawkins, Indian agent for Central Alabama Creek Territory, reported riding by horseback to the farm of Robert Grierson, located in the area of the Hillabee tribe of the Creek Indians near Hackneyville:

> *He* [Grierson] *had a treadle gin sent him from Providence…three years after Eli Whitney had invented the cotton gin….He hired Indian women to pick out cotton….Upon Hawkins' recommendation, he set up a manufactory of cotton cloth; he plants seed cotton it being too cold for black seed. He raised a quantity for market, but finds it more profitable to manufacture it, he has employed an active girl of Georgia, Rachael Spillard, who was in the Cherokee Department, to superintendent eleven hands, red, white, and black, in spinning and weaving, and the other part of his family is raising and preparing the cotton for him.*[107]

Little is known about the development of Grierson's manufacturing enterprise, but a little more than a decade later, the Native American tribes had split into the Lower Creeks and the Upper Creeks. Tallapoosa and nearby counties were Upper Creeks. Tension built with the arrival of traders, pioneers and military until the War of 1812 began a series of battles, ending in Andrew Jackson's defeat of the Great Creek Nation at the Battle of Horseshoe Bend in March 1814. With the forfeiting of land and power, the Native Americans lost any opportunity to thrive in manufacturing cotton cloth or even farming cotton fields. The life they lived for hundreds of years had ended.

INTERVIEW WITH BEN RUSSELL

> *During his lifetime Mr. Russell, the young man from a farm in one of the poorest and most rural areas of the South, had created a bank, a textile mill, a development potential of hundreds of miles of prime shoreline, an entire farming community, a mill village, church, school, hospital, a phone company, a municipal water supply, a foundry, a woodworking industry, a hotel, a dairy, a bakery, a soft drink bottling company, a laundry, a wholesale grocery and founded the State Chamber of Commerce.*[108]

In 1902, Benjamin Russell began operation of his knitting mill in a fifty-by-one-hundred-foot wooden building with six knitting machines and ten sewing machines.

ALEXANDER CITY'S TEXTILE MILLS

The first chapters of Central Alabama history begin with Native Americans, while they were still living on their ancestral lands, hunting, fishing and trading furs. The traders came first to live in the wilderness alongside the Indians, often marrying Indian women and establishing families with mixed blood. The kinship made it possible for the traders to move freely within the Creek Nation. As settlers moved into Creek and Cherokee land, the tension between the two ethnic groups heightened and culminated in defeat of the Creeks at the Battle of Horseshoe Bend in March 1814. Nothing could stop the influx of white settlers nor the discriminatory application of treaty terms. The government broke each treaty and used every opportunity to lay claim to acres of farmland—in some instances, while Indian families still lived in cabins with gardens nearby. Andrew Jackson's Indian Removal Act dealt the final blow to those Indians who remained and fought in the last skirmishes between the Creeks and the Tennessee Militia. They were forced to march to Oklahoma in 1836 in brutal weather with little food or clothing to protect them. Thousands of Native Americans died as federal soldiers forced them along what became known as the Trail of Tears.

Settlement in Central Alabama began with pioneer families crossing the old Federal Road from South Carolina and Georgia into Alabama. In 1836, there were a few ferries that could carry the heavy burden of wagons, families, horses and other farm animals across rivers. James Young and his large family rode a ferry across the Tallapoosa River. James stopped at Tuckabatchee, once the site of the Creek confederacy, and told his family, "Here is our new home." He established a store known as the Georgia Trading Post on the land previously owned by the Creeks. As more members of the Young family arrived and built homes near the post, the "town" became known as Youngsville. When the city was incorporated as Youngsville in 1872, the members of the Young family held prominent positions as mayors, lawyers, judges and educators. The most famous was Bird Young, who was Tallapoosa County's first census taker, in 1840, and the inspiration for Hooper's character Simon Suggs. Author, editor and lawyer Johnson Jones Hooper stayed at the Dennis hotel in Dadeville, where lawyers gathered and exchanged stories. Hooper's character Simon Suggs was mischievous and possessed natural wit that allowed him to best others in his "business dealings." The book *Simon Suggs Adventures* is a collection of stories about Suggs, whose character is mirrored in Mark Twain's equally conniving character "King" in *Huckleberry Finn*. Due to the Civil War, completion of the railroad track was delayed until 1873, when the Savannah and Memphis Railway came to Youngsville. The engine bore the name *Simon Suggs*. The town was renamed Alexander City in 1874, in honor of S&M Railroad president Edward P. Alexander. In 1874, the arrival of the first train brought opportunities for travel, mail delivery, shipping and receiving merchandise for stores.

The first mill in Alexander City, the Alexander City Manufacturing Company, began production in the 1890s. On June 13, 1902, the progress the town had made in establishing churches, homes and businesses was lost in a fire that started in a livery stable and swept through Broad Street and reduced the town to ashes. Even the railroad tracks were destroyed. Farmers brought their equipment to help clear rubbish. People from neighboring towns donated money and labor. The Opelika newspaper publisher provided temporary use of its printing equipment to publish Alexander City news. Where possible, brick was used to replace wooden structures. The town established fire ordinances and organized a fire department to extinguish the

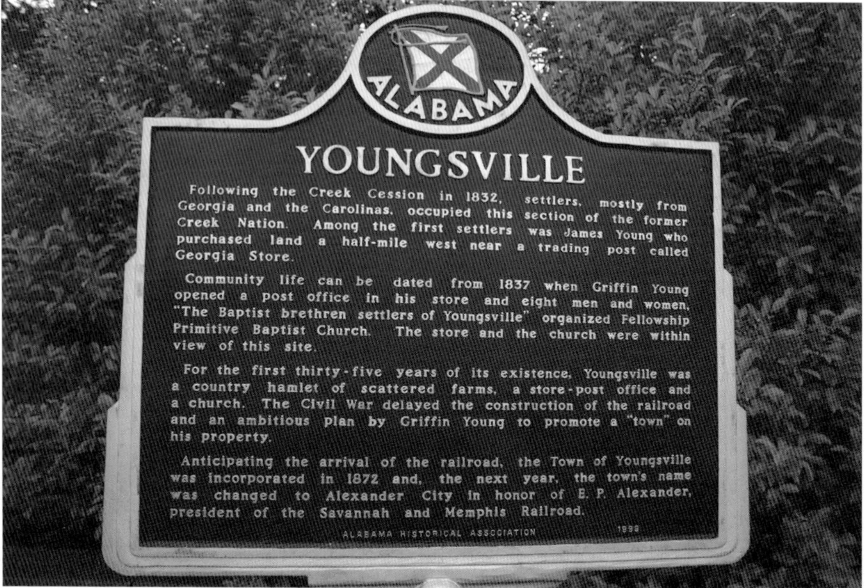

James Young established a trading post on land formerly owned by the Creek Nation at Tuckabatchee, near Alexander City, Tallapoosa County. *Youngsville AHA Marker.*

flames of a fire. An optimistic forecast for the town's economic growth came in April 1902, when Benjamin Russell started a small textile mill in a fifty-by-one-hundred-foot building, surrounded by 320 acres of land for future expansion. There were six knitting machines and ten sewing machines. The first items the seamstresses produced were ladies and children's underwear—a humble beginning for the mill that became the world's largest producer of athletic wear.

Over the span of a few years, Russell Manufacturing expanded into the town's largest employer. The Russell family supported local organizations and businesses and established Russell Hospital in 1923 with thirty-five beds. Benjamin Russell High School opened its doors in September 1950 to welcome students from the old Alexander City School and the Bevelle School. The school was built without state or federal money. It was totally funded by the Russell Educational and Charitable Foundation, Avondale Mills and donations from local businessmen. Mr. Robert Russell named the school after his father, Benjamin Russell. The Black community's school, Laurel, and Benjamin Russell merged in 1971, seventeen years after the U.S. Supreme Court ruled the policy of "separate but equal" schools was unconstitutional. Other businesses owned or managed by a member of

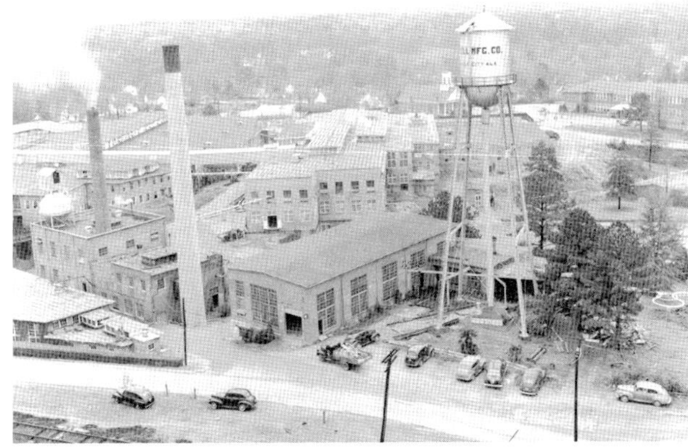

Russell manufacturing company. Russell plant office beside the railroad track, with water tank, schools, church and mill village in the background. *Robert Graves collection.*

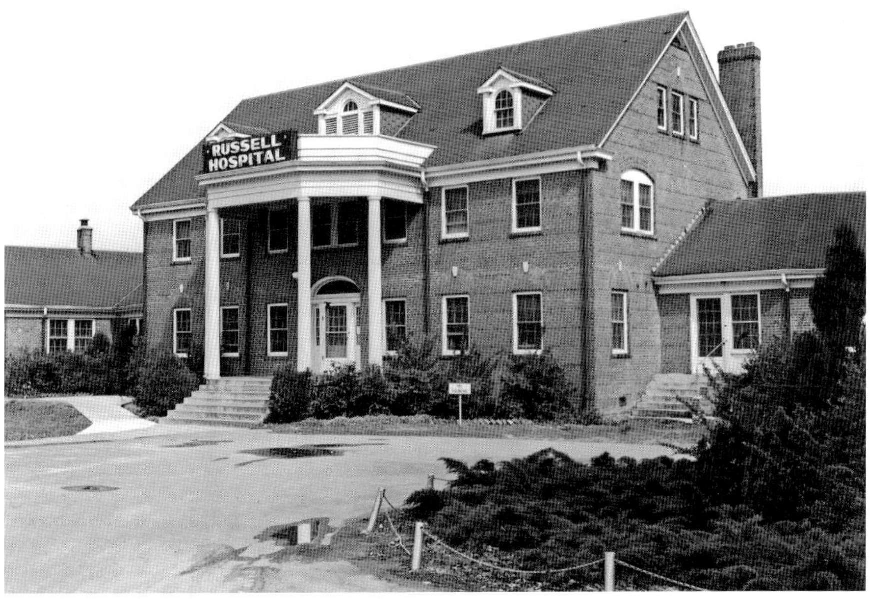

Russell Hospital. In 1923, the Russell family built Alexander City's first hospital, serving the community with a thirty-five-bed capacity. *Robert Graves collection.*

the Russell family included the First National Bank. Benjamin Russell was president of the board. His brother, Thomas Commander Russell, was elected mayor for the first of ten terms, serving from 1907 to 1947. The city library, built in 1965, was named in honor of Adelia Russell.

The company began its operations in spinning in 1908, woven cloth in 1923, bleaching in 1931 and athletic apparel in 1912 or '13. Electricity replaced steam as the primary source of power in 1912. Many of the

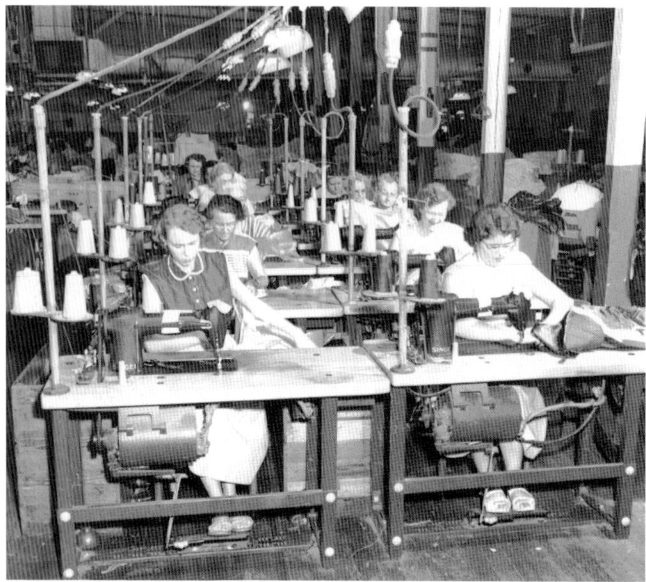

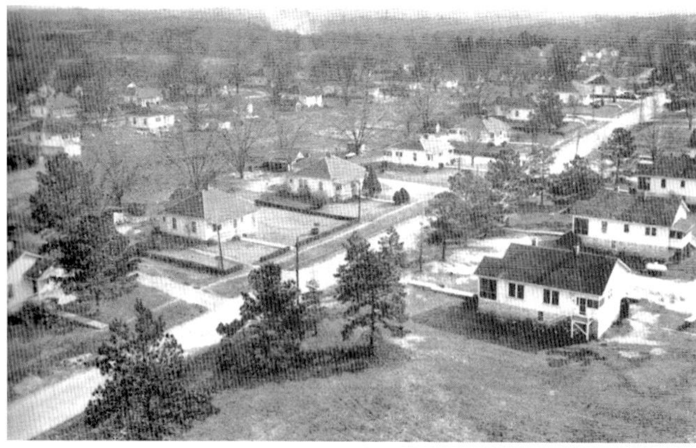

Top: Ladies sewing at machines at Russell manufacturing, working on production, circa 1948. Any number of shirts over the required earned extra pay. *Robert Graves collection.*

Bottom: Russell Mill Village. In the 1950s, the mill houses were torn down and the lumber was used to build cabins on Lake Martin. *Robert Graves collection.*

employees who worked at Russell lived on farms and could not easily travel back and forth to work in the early years of mill production. Like other textile mills, the Russell Company built mill villages where workers could pay a modest rent and live near the plant. Amenities like the Russell swimming pool, churches, schools and company-sponsored events like annual barbecues added to the benefit of living in town.

By the 1950s and '60s, the homes were disassembled and moved to Kowaliga, where the materials were used to build lake cabins in a small park near Kowaliga Bridge. A few of the tiny green cabins remain as reminders of the time when life was simpler and lake real estate much less expensive.

Wind Creek Lake and surrounding land were developed into a state park, replacing the smaller facilities at Kowaliga. The forty thousand acres of Lake Martin now is located in three counties: Tallapoosa, Elmore and Coosa.

> *The company evolved over the next century into an international apparel concern with more than $1 billion in annual sales and more than 15,000 employees worldwide. After 20 years as a publicly traded company, in 2006 Russell Corporation became a wholly owned subsidiary of Berkshire Hathaway, a multinational holding company chaired by billionaire Warren Buffet.*[109]

Avondale Mill Village

Alexander City was home to two major textile mills, Russell and Avondale. In the early 1900s, small cotton mills operated throughout East Central Alabama. Many failed, but after struggling at the beginning, Russell and Avondale prospered and employed thousands of workers at a time when jobs were scarce. The textile mills were the economic core of the mill towns. In addition to providing jobs, they supported city institutions and built churches and schools. Avondale Mills based many decisions on how investments might benefit the working families as well as the corporate investors and management. The Avondale Mills had a humble beginning, dependent on eastern capital and wealthy investors in the state. The Trainer family from Chester, Pennsylvania, established Avondale Mills in Birmingham in 1897. Eastern investors purchased stock to finance the building and equipping of the mill. Braxton Bragg Comer took $10,000 worth of stock and became president of Avondale Mills corporation. With a small staff, he worked until the mill was stable. In 1907, when he became governor of Alabama, he transferred management of the two mills that were in existence at the time to his sons Donald and Fletcher. In 1912, Eva Jane Mill was built in Sylacauga. Avondale had five plants in the county. On June 22, 2011, the Eva Jane plant caught fire and burned to the ground. In 1919, Avondale acquired mills in Alexander City, Sycamore and Pell City, making a total of eight mills at the time. Avondale purchased the old Alexander City Cotton Mill and changed the name to Bevelle in honor of a younger daughter of Braxton Bragg Comer. Many plants were named in honor of Comer women. The Eva Jane plant was named for B.B. Comer's wife. Other plants were named

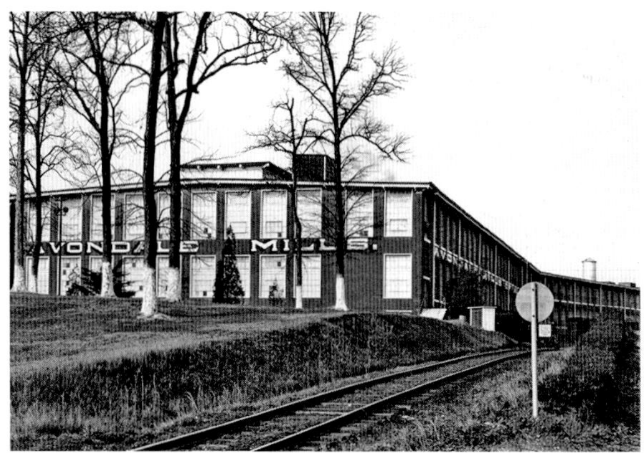

Avondale Mills opened a textile plant in Alexander City in 1918. In 2006, Parkdale Mills purchased the plant, named Bevelle, saving two hundred jobs. *Alabama Department of Archives and History.*

for Comer's children: Catherine, Sallie B. and Mignon. In the early years of production, Avondale plants typically turned out rope, hosiery yarns, sheeting, indigo denims and heavy twills. In the 1940s, favorite materials were seersucker for suits, dresses and children's clothes; wide chambray; yarns; thread in large cones; and ticking for mattresses. Avondale Mills was the world's largest producer of ticking. The items in the Avondale cloth store were sold only to employees and their families.[110]

Most plants provided mill villages, where workers could live within walking distance of their jobs. Amenities included lots for vegetable gardens and a cannery to preserve food for winter months. Workers paid seventy-five cents a week for housing out of a salary of twelve to twenty dollars a week. The mill village had a dairy and a poultry farm; there were two large churches, the Methodist and the Comer Memorial Baptist Church; a dentist; and doctor offices. Other buildings included a recreational building, Byers baseball field, a Boy Scouts cabin and the J. Fletcher and Helen B. Memorial swimming pool built by Bevelle employees, friends and citizens of Alexander City to honor the couple. Red Cross gave swimming lessons, culminating at the end of summer with a water show.

The annual barbecue for employees and their families started in the 1920s and continued into the mid-1900s. After annual inspections, company plant officials and workers were entertained by the Bevelle school band and an operetta performed by Ms. Holbrook's students. Across the railroad from the plant, a strip of stores included a beauty shop, grocery store, shoe repair shop and drugstore.[111]

Braxton Bragg Comer operated a large plantation before becoming president of Avondale Mills and governor of the state of Alabama. Comer was criticized for running the mills like he did his plantation. He met the workers' needs by providing not just a job but also social functions, religious organizations and recreational activities. Most of the poor whites and Blacks who came from sharecropping and working from "sun-up to sun-down" appreciated the regular wage paid by their textile job. During the 1930s and '40s, union organizers came into the South and tried to organize unions at Avondale and Russell Mills. But workers enjoyed the amenities that B.B. Comer and the Avondale plant provided, and when union organizers came to Bevelle, stood at the gate and handed out flyers, workers had little interest in starting a union. The manager of the plant announced to the workers that if they tried to start a union, the plant would be shut down immediately and everyone would lose their job. Not everyone was afraid that would happen, and some were not afraid of working to establish unions at the mills in East Central Alabama. J.P. Mooney worked as a driller in the Hog Mountain gold mine in the 1930s and organized a strike when management refused to rotate shifts to give men a break in working the third shift all the time.[112]

After meeting with resistance, Mooney and the other men were successful in attaining their demands. In 1939, after the gold mines were closed, he joined the International Union of Mine, Mill and Smelter Workers at the steel mills around Fairfield and Ensley. Then he went to work for the United Textile Workers of America. He oversaw unionizing mills in the Southeast, mainly Alexander City, Sylacauga and Opelika. He waged an unsuccessful campaign before serving in the Merchant Marine. Upon his return, the few men who had become involved in the attempts to organize a union had lost their jobs. After CIO and AFL sued Avondale Mills, Russell Mills and other East Central Alabama textile mills, the workers were reinstated. Organizers were permitted to distribute flyers and hold meetings without harassment or fear of losing their jobs. The attempts to organize unions were unsuccessful, in part due to the workers' loyalty to the Comer and Russell families. A great deal of violence occurred in the '30s and '40s as workers and management clashed in other southern states.

Camp Helen was a company resort located west of Panama City Beach, south of U.S. 98 and bounded by the Gulf of Mexico and Lake Powell. From 1945 to 1987, Avondale rotated the closing of plants so that employees of each plant could take a week's vacation to swim and beachcomb. The weekly fee to stay in a cabin room and eat three meals a day was thirteen dollars. The camp is known now as Camp Helen State Park and was entered in the National Register of Historic Places on May 24, 2012. B.B. Comer provided amenities that employees enjoyed, and because of that, they had little reason to strike for changes. They had churches, medical and dental services at a

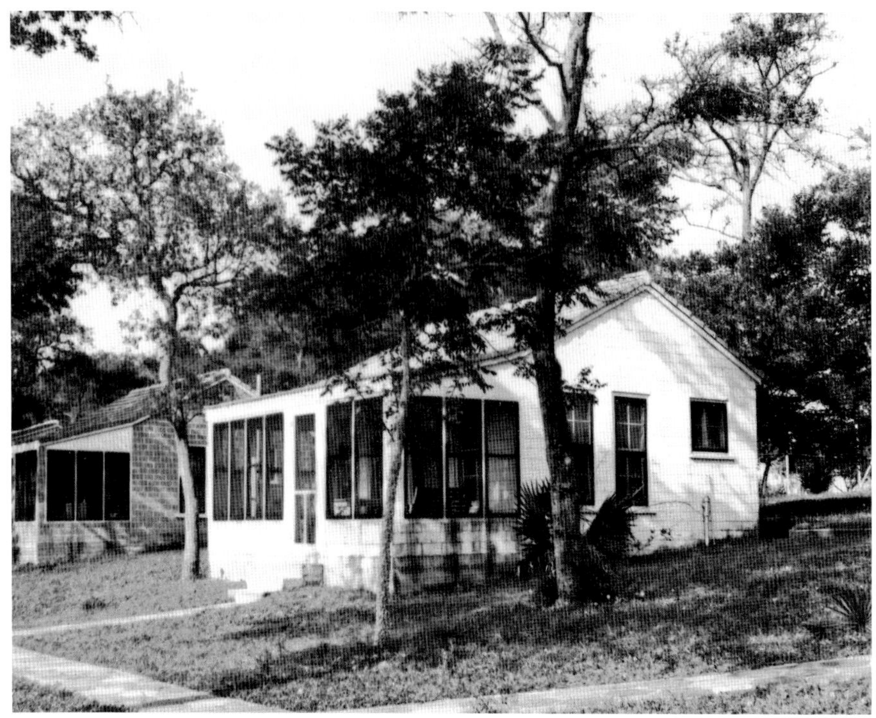

Camp Helen. Avondale rotated the closing of plants, providing employees of each plant a week's vacation, swimming and beachcombing. *Robert Graves collection.*

reduced price. They had opportunity to participate in sports, swimming, arts programs, entertainment, a week's vacation in the summer, access to sports programs and a band. Byers ball field was named for superintendent Jimmy Byers. The Avondale baseball team practiced and played teams from other Avondale Mills on the field. Alexander City's first organized Black baseball team was composed of Bevelle employees called Black Crackers. One of the big games they played and won was against the Birmingham Barons and Willie Mays.[113]

Despite the goodwill generated by the company's amenities, B.B. Comer received criticism for using child labor extensively and opposing legislation that prohibited hiring underage workers. Some families objected to child labor; others welcomed the chance for additional family income. Comer justified the use of child labor by stating that some parents demanded that children be permitted to work. However, this argument did not diminish the fact that conditions were dangerous. Children were expected to work long hours. They had little opportunity to attend school. Still, legislation was slow

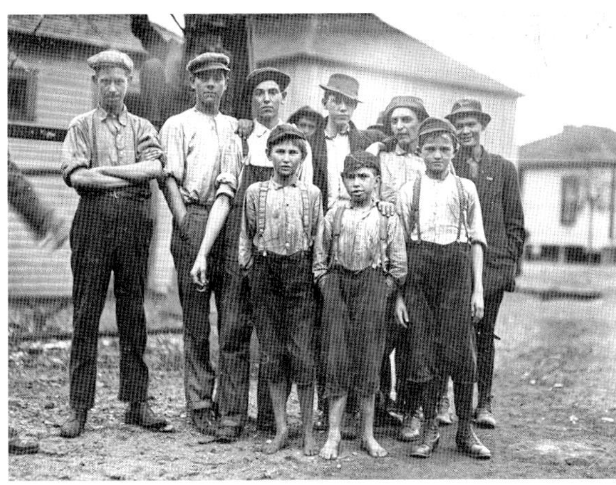

Child laborers pose on the Avondale Mills property for photographer and social reformer Lewis Hines during the early twentieth century. *National Child Labor Committee, courtesy of the Library of Congress.*

in coming to restrict textile mills' use of child labor. In 1938, child labor laws required that young people's work be safe from physical harm.[114]

Avondale Mills remained in operation when other companies were selling or reducing the number of employees. It was optimistic in continuing its 161-year operation. The disastrous train wreck in Graniteville, South Carolina, in January 2005 ended those plans. CEO Stephen Felker Sr., chairman and president, announced the closing of Avondale Mills:

> *Citing unfair global competition exacerbated by a disastrous train derailment in January 2005 outside one of its plants in Graniteville, S.C., Monroe, Ga.–based Avondale Mills Inc. has closed its doors after 161 years of operation. The closure affects 4,000 associates—many representing the second, third, fourth or even fifth generation of their families to have worked for the company—at its various facilities in Georgia, Alabama and South Carolina….But the train accident, which caused a chlorine spill that took the lives of several Avondale associates and caused insurmountable damage to the plant, ultimately derailed the company itself. As Felker also wrote in his letter: "We have worked hard for a year and a half to recover, but the damage is too great. Without the train derailment and chemical spill, we were challenged. With it, we were destroyed."*[115]
>
> *From its founding in 1897, textile manufacturing firm Avondale Mills left its mark on towns and cities throughout Alabama. Avondale Mills earned the respect of many mill workers for its Progressive Era programs for employees, and the disdain of reformers for its labor practices, particularly the use of child labor. Avondale Mills spanned the rise and fall*

of Alabama's industrial history, and its most notable owners, the Comer family, became some of the most powerful people in the state. The company ceased operations in July 2006, unable to compete with foreign textile manufacturers and unable to recover from a tragic train accident next to its Graniteville, South Carolina, facility in 2005.[116]

PEPPERELL MILLS

Every business begins with the goal of achieving financial success for the company and its employees. Pepperell Manufacturing Company held this goal when it constructed a mill village between 1925 and 1940.[117] The village provided homes to the workers, where they were close enough to walk to work and to hear the mill whistle at the changing of shifts. The Pepperell Mill made a strong impact on local businesses in Opelika and surrounding areas. Like other mill villages in Alabama, the textile company established communities where work, social, school and church activities united the people. The village began with approximately 100 houses; by 1946, there were approximately 240 buildings. Besides the homes, the community had a post office, church, school, childcare facility, drugstore, barbershop, gas station and grocery store. In 1958, the company began selling the house lots to individual owners. The mill continued to operate until 2006.[118]

In April 1925, ground was broken in a former cotton field, and construction began on the mill and 100 houses, as Pepperell Mill Village became reality. The mill was completed in 1926 with the first yard of cloth woven on Feb. 25. The school opened in September with around 200 students. A church was constructed for Baptist and Methodist congregations. In 1927, a grocery store, barbershop and theatre were built, with the theatre closing a few years later to enlarge the grocery store and add a drug store. A baseball and athletic field were built in the village in 1930 and the Lady Pepperell Shop in 1933. In the years that followed, the mill village was home to hundreds of families and countless children who grew up playing with friends after school and meeting at the drugstore for a cold drink. These stories are about happy times and hardships families faced during those days.[119]

Pepperell Mills became famous as the filming site for the award-winning film *Norma Rae*, based on the true story of Crystal Lee Sutton, first told in

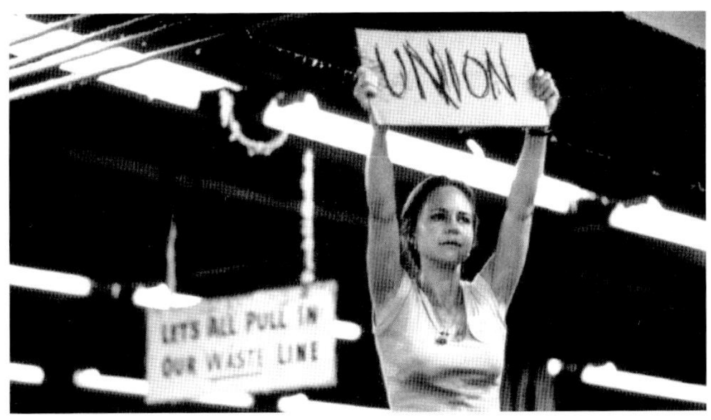

Sallie Fields in the award-winning movie *Norma Rae*, filmed at Pepperell Mills in Opelika, Alabama. She holds the sign "Union" for workers to respond to by shutting off their machines. *Amazon.*

the 1975 book *Crystal Lee, a Woman of Inheritance*. The book was made into a screenplay written by Irving Ravetch and Harriet Frank Jr. Sallie Fields played the role of Norma Rae, an uneducated millworker who, with others, attempted to organize a union in 1979. Grievances against the company were poor working conditions, unhealthy environment and inadequate pay. The film's most iconic and well-known scene is the moment when Norma Rae stands on a table at the mill and holds up a sign that reads "Union." One by one, the workers around her stop their machines, and silence falls on the factory floor. Norma Rae was arrested and taken to jail but released to Rueben, a union organizer. In real life, main character Sallie Fields struggled so hard with the police officers in the scene that she broke a rib.[120]

The brick structure and the tall chimney were treasured sights to the people who lived in the Pepperell Mill Village across the street. The sight of the mill burning on the night of March 12, 2013, was shocking to people who lived nearby. The news of the tragedy spread rapidly, reaching people in Opelika and other communities. The shared memories of hundreds of mill hands and families who once worked there created a bond that would not be destroyed by fire. The mill village was left intact. The social events continued in the two churches in the village and community. Homes remain attractive and reminiscent of another era. The mill and village are now in the National Register of Historic Places. "The architecture of the buildings in the village are representative examples of textile mill residential and industrial. Standardized mill housing included Craftsman/Bungalow style details, common folk forms like gable fronts, pyramidal, and massed plan variations....Before the fire, the new owner had planned to turn the mill into residential housing, she [Lisa Harrelson, Opelika's historic preservation coordinator] said."[121] The fire destroyed the plant

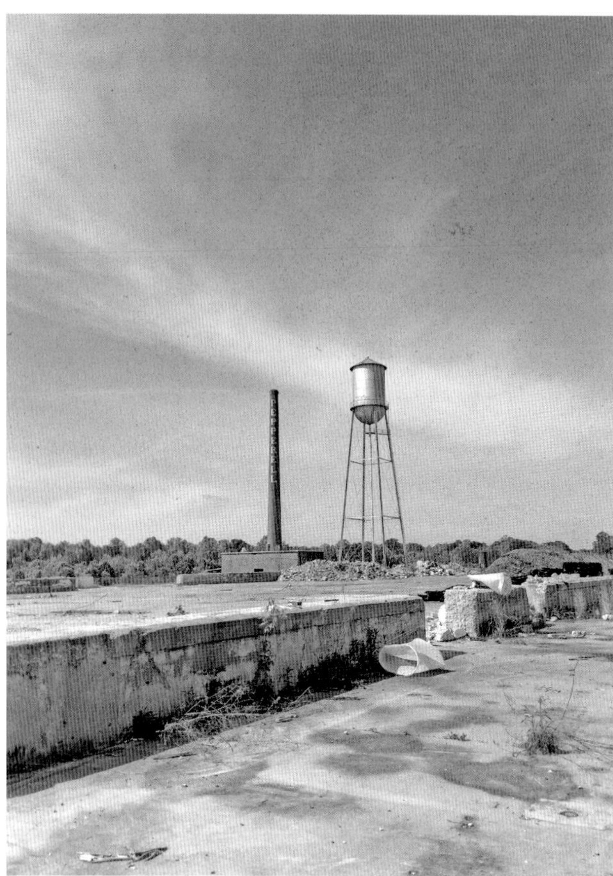

Left: On March 12, 2013, fire swept through Pepperell Mills. It burned the buildings but spared the chimney and the mill village across the street. *Author's collection.*

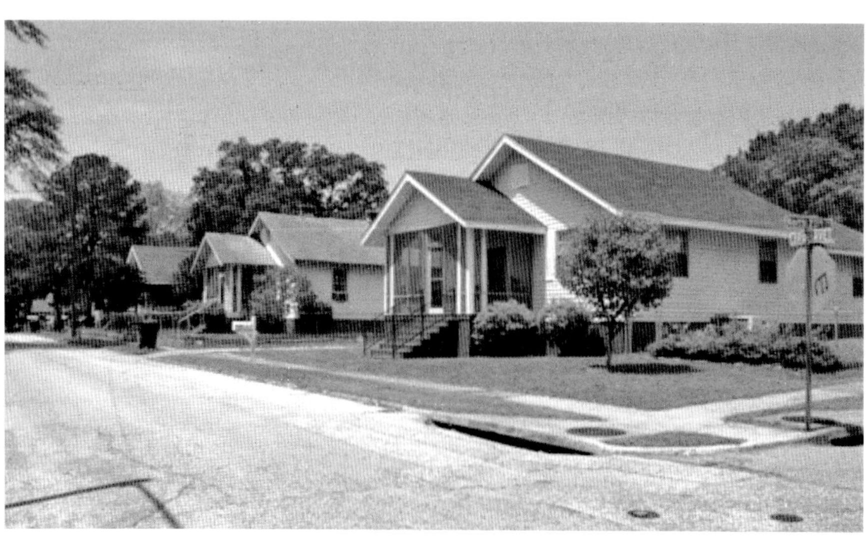

Below: Pepperell Mills was destroyed by fire, but the village survived. The mill village and the mill property are in the National Register of Historic Places. *Courtesy National Park Service.*

and swept away everything but memories. The village is reminiscent of earlier days when neighbors sat in the front porch swing and watched children play ball, sometimes walking across the street to the pavilion and picnic area in the Pepperell Park.

Tallassee Mills and Village

Textile mills in Tallassee were in operation as early as the 1840s. Tallassee Falls Manufacturing Company began producing cotton cloth and, later, wool cloth. As forecasted by Benjamin Hawkins, the falls would make the location a successful industrial site. Use of Tallassee Falls to power the plant kept the mill at the core of Tallassee's economy for approximately 160 years. In the mid-1850s, the mills were operated by Barnett, Gilmer and Company. During the Civil War, the Tallassee Guards became Confederate soldiers. Union soldiers attempted two unsuccessful raids on the arms manufacturing facility located in Tallassee. Due to the town's isolation, railroad lines did not run through Tallassee until 1896. The same year, a dam was built across the Tallapoosa River to provide water to the mill and the town. In 1900, the Tallassee Falls Manufacturing Company became part of the Mount Vernon–Woodberry Cotton Duck Company. The opening of a Tallassee school system in 1950 was followed in the same year by a fire that damaged buildings downtown.[122]

Old Tallassee was laid out in about 1835 on the eastern side of the Tallapoosa River. The second Tallassee town was developed on property owned by Barent DuBois on both sides of the river. He was credited with being the first white man to utilize the power of the falls to operate a gristmill and sawmill. DuBois was born in Catskills, New York. At the age of twenty-two, he traveled to Alabama and served as an Indian agent at Tukabahachee, where he met and married a Creek woman named Milly. Thomas Meriwether Barnett (1785–1857) and William Matthews Marks (1807–1876), of Montgomery County, Alabama, purchased property from DuBois on the west side of the river. By the end of 1844, they had constructed a mill in a small stone building.[123]

> *The workers for the mill lived in a small village also on the west side of the river. In 1850 over 90% of the mill employees could not read and write and apparently there was no attempt to provide schools for their children.*

Children worked long hours in the mill alongside their parents. Barnett probably supervised the workers himself and may have ridden by horseback to Tallassee each morning. In 1844, except for the little mill village, there was no town as such on the west side of the river. Above and beyond the river at the falls the country was settled by farmers....

In the early 1900's, wells provided the new village of East Tallassee with water. These were in the street where several families had equal access to them. Every family had its own cows and hogs for milk and meat. Josh DuBois was the herdsman for the village. He went out each morning herding the cows to pasture. He returned them in the afternoon to their owners. Likewise, each family had a small pen or barn....Hogs were allowed to run free....The hogs found the unpenned Baptist Church a good place to sleep, especially in winter months. On occasion they made so much noise the service had to be discontinued until the hogs were chased from under the church. The village houses were heated by wood or coal and lighted with kerosene lamps. A large coal yard was maintained in back of the company store. In 1912, running water was installed on the back porch of the unscreened village houses....Employees worked a twelve-hour shift for five days a week and until eleven o'clock and resumed at 1 o'clock to allow children to carry baskets of lunch to their parents and others working in the mill. The children were paid five cents per lunch per day.[124]

Progress was significant when the dams were completed, making electricity possible to businesses. Alabama Power completed Thurlow Dam on December 31, 1930. Local historian Bill Goss observed, "Thurlow Dam created Lake Talisi with a shoreline of six miles and an area of 574 acres." Although the Tallassee Mills were able to keep operating during the Great Depression, they ran on reduced schedules, enabling the town of Tallassee and businesses to survive. The four dams on the Tallapoosa River—Martin, Yates, Thurlow and Harris—supplied electricity to the entire Southeast.[125]

In 1900, the Tallassee facility became part of Mount Vernon Mills. In the 1940s, the Tallassee Mills received the Army-Navy "E" Award from the U.S. government for excellence and efficiency in the production of war materials. In World War I and World War II, Tallassee supplied the United States with duck cloth for tents, sails and cots. On May 5, 2016, Tallassee Mills burned and was a total loss. It was a tragic event for the hundreds of people who had worked in the mill and for their descendants. The Tallassee Mills were the oldest continuously operating mills in the United States, providing 161 years of service in Central Alabama.[126]

Maple Hill Cemetery

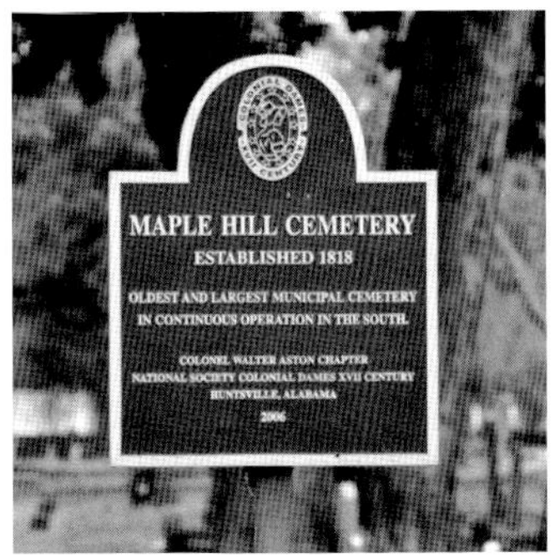

Maple Hill is a large, haunted cemetery famous for the sounds of children playing and other spooky stories that include graves of former governors. *"Dead Children's Playground," Onlyinyourstate.com/alabama/maple-hill-cemetery-al.*

Maple Hill is a resting place for some of Alabama's high-ranking politicians, including five U.S. senators (John Williams Walker, Clement Comer Clay, Jeremiah Clemens, Clement Claiborne Clay and John Sparkman) and five Alabama governors (Thomas Bibb, Clement Comer Clay, Reuben Chapman, Robert Patton and David Lewis).

Upon his brother William Wyatt Bibb's death on July 10, 1820, Thomas Bibb, then president of the Alabama Senate, was placed in the governor's office, as specified by the state constitution, on July 15, 1820. When Thomas and his wife discussed where they should be buried upon their deaths, they disagreed. She was a socialite and liked the idea of being buried at the Maple Hill Cemetery, where so many notable people were buried. Thomas, on the other hand, wanted to be buried on the grounds of his Belle Manor in Limestone County. Thomas lost the debate, so when he died, he was buried in Huntsville's oldest and largest cemetery. Despite the prestige of being among other governors and senators, there seemed to be no rest for Thomas. Among the numerous ghost stories of Maple Hill Cemetery is the account of Thomas reputedly seen on nights with a full moon leaving his crypt and entering a carriage. He drives about the cemetery searching for the way home to his beloved Belle Manor.

Mary Chambers Bibb

Mary was the daughter-in-law of Thomas Bibb. The story begins with her accidental poisoning by one of her servants. She died in May 1835 after suffering for months. The family wanted a special tomb for her that she might have chosen for herself. They built the first mausoleum in Maple Hill Cemetery. It was large enough to hold her and a rocking chair. The mausoleum was a favorite place for curious children. They would rush to the crypt, knock on the wall and stand trembling at the sound of Mary's rocking chair moving in answer to their knock.

Dead Children's Playground

Several stories circulate about the playground found in the cemetery. One is that there were a series of abductions and murders of children in the 1960s; however, no data has ever been offered to substantiate this claim. But proof is not necessary for a good ghost story, just a good imagination. Another version of the same story attributes the many deaths of the children to the Spanish flu in 1918. Whether either story is true, a large number of children are buried in the Maple Hill Cemetery. There is a playground where children are welcome, whether as visitors or from among those who remain in the cemetery. Visitors have reported hearing children's giggling and observed swings moving on their own. With so many rather prominent elderly people buried at Maple Hill, it must be refreshing to hear those happy sounds and, of course, the squeaking of the swings as they carry the invisible children off the ground into the air.

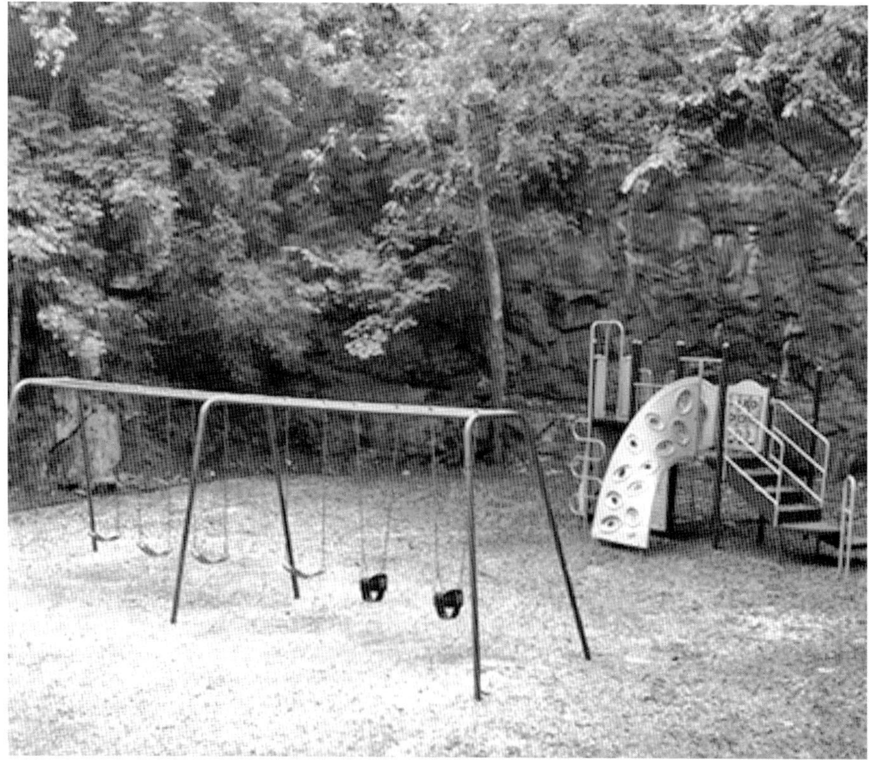

Visitors to the Maple Hill Cemetery may see swings moving and hear the laughter of children playing in an area called the Dead Children's Playground. *Facebook*.

Dexter Avenue

On January 30, 1879, the First Baptist Church congregation in Montgomery purchased a 50-by-110-foot lot and the small wood frame building on it. Between 1883 and 1889, the structure was replaced with the current red brick building. Located on the corner of Dexter Avenue and Decatur Street near the capitol building, the church met the community's worship and educational needs. Registration of students for the Normal School for Colored Students, now Alabama State University, was held in the lower unit of the church on October 3, 1887.

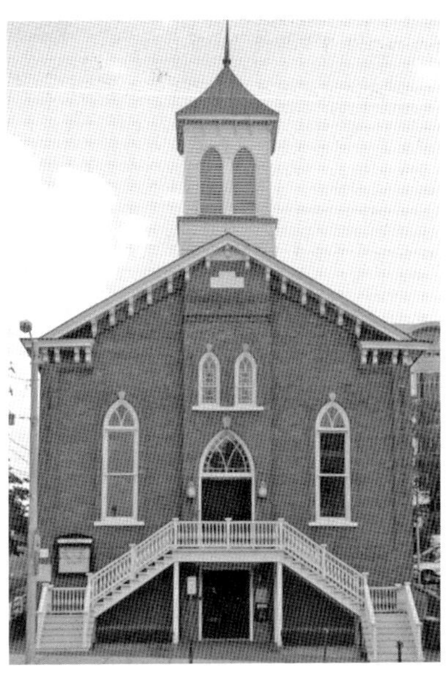

The Dexter Avenue King Memorial Baptist Church was founded in 1877 in a slave trader's pen located on Dexter Avenue (formerly Market Street) in Montgomery, Alabama. *Dexter Avenue King Memorial Baptist Church.*

The church's name was changed to Dexter in honor of the city founder, Andrew Dexter. The final change was made in 1978 to Dexter Avenue King Memorial Baptist Church. The church was the center of Montgomery's early civil rights activity. The twentieth pastor, Dr. Martin Luther King Jr., directed the 1956 bus boycott from his office in the church, where he was pastor from 1954 to 1960. On July 13, 1976, Montgomery added Dexter Church to its list of historic sites; in 1982, the church was placed in the National Register of Historic Places. A ten-by-forty-seven-foot mural, painted by Deacon John W. Feagin, illustrates events of the civil rights movement at Dexter Avenue King Memorial Baptist Church. The church and mural attract thousands of national and international visitors annually.

Slave Depots

In antebellum years, Montgomery had four major slave depots, three on Market Street (now Dexter Avenue). Mason Hartwell, S.N. Brown and E.

Barnard & Co. owned depots that lined Market Street between Lawrence and McDonough. In 1859, in Montgomery's slave market, slave owners in a single day sold hundreds of slaves. Montgomery's location was convenient for the slave owners to transport their slaves on the river and unload them at the dock. They were then marched up Commerce Street and auctioned off on the Court Square. Montgomery had as many slave depots as hotels and banks. Enslaved men, women and children were auctioned alongside livestock.

THE EQUAL JUSTICE INITIATIVE

The Equal Justice Initiative (EJI) is committed to ending mass incarceration and excessive punishment in the United States, to challenging racial and economic injustice and to protecting basic human rights for the most vulnerable people in American society.

Founded in 1989 by Bryan Stevenson, a widely acclaimed public interest lawyer and best-selling author of *Just Mercy*, EJI is a private 501(c)(3) nonprofit organization. It is located at 122 Commerce Street in Montgomery. EJI works with communities that have been marginalized by poverty and discouraged by unequal treatment.

The organization is dedicated to helping the poor, the incarcerated and the condemned by providing legal assistance to innocent death row prisoners, confronting abuse of the incarcerated and the mentally ill and aiding children prosecuted as adults. EJI is actively engaged in a campaign to recognize the victims of lynching by collecting soil from lynching sites, erecting historical markers and creating a national memorial that acknowledges the horrors of racial injustice.

Set on a six-acre site, the National Memorial for Peace and Justice and the Legacy Museum opened on April 18, 2018. One of the many purposes of the EJI is to document the thousands of racial terror lynchings in twelve states. Each of the eight hundred six-foot monuments is a symbol of the racial terror lynching, listing the counties and states where the lynchings took place. Names of the victims are engraved on the columns.

The museum and memorial are two separate sites, about 0.7 miles apart. The Legacy Museum is an indoor narrative museum with exhibits, art and narratives about the legacy of enslavement through contemporary issues. The National Memorial is an outdoor memorial with a path where visitors can walk and view the history of racial injustice.

AFTERWORD

Old towns cling to the past—dilapidated buildings, tall weeds covering what was once a well-tended yard, an abandoned orchard in back. The families who inhabited these houses, built businesses and filled houses of worship moved to communities with more options for work and improvement of their circumstances. Rich farming land enticed settlers to establish their farms in Central Alabama. When cotton was king, the hard work of farming yielded prosperity to many. After the Civil War and emancipation of slaves, the economy remained agrarian, but many of the large plantations in the Black Belt counties fell into disrepair. Farms depended on the help of sharecropper tenants whose wages kept them in bondage. The core of the economy remained cotton, but labor changed from working in cotton fields to working in cotton mills producing sweatshirts, T-shirts and other cotton clothing. Entire families left their farms and moved to mill villages to work as mill hands. A regular income, even if small, was better than depending on an unpredictable crop. When railroads came through towns, they brought prosperity, products and machinery. When they left, they took with them the opportunity for local people to ship their goods to larger markets. Finally, railroads were dismantled and removed, leaving the local people with little opportunity to expand their businesses or even to travel by train.

Much is forgotten about the small towns that once were well populated and teeming with life. As older people die, memories of the ghost towns inevitably pass too unless stories are repeated and recorded. The stories that people tell, the memories they share make the communities and the people real to new generations. Many towns were founded with dreams that eventually became outdated. At some point, dreams were not enough to sustain the people or save the town. Stores closed, and residents moved. Historical markers and county histories record names and events peculiar to a place and time. Stories remain with the people whose ancestors lived in the ghost towns. Discovering the people and gathering the information is an effort like those extended by archaeologists who dig in sites to discover what they can about the past, how they lived, descriptions of their dwellings and the people.

Lost Towns of Central Alabama begins with the first Americans and the first accounts of Europeans. Archaeologists have unearthed information about the large and important town of Mabila. De Soto's chroniclers recorded a description of the town and the people, including the encounter with Hernando de Soto and Chief Tuskaloosa, who is described as a seven-foot man of great strength and dignity.

The ghost towns leave a legacy, like the town of Benson, which was built and sustained through the efforts of former slaves and their families with financial assistance from northern philanthropic organizations. During the years of KKK activity referenced in the Benson story, the largest sharecroppers' union in Alabama was located in Tallapoosa County. Nathan Shaw, a Black sharecropper, told his story to a graduate student, Theodore Rosengarten, who interviewed Shaw as part of his master's thesis and later incorporated the story into the award-winning book *All God's Dangers*, winner of the National Book Award in 1975.

Bob Saxon, editor of *The 125th Anniversary of Alexander City* and dean of education at a local community college, wrote about the Youngsville Klan burning the New Elam church where the sharecroppers' union met. In addition to the church burning, the Klan rode into the members' yards, threatening and terrorizing them. A common practice was to tell the farmer to get on the ground. He was then measured for his coffin and told when and where his funeral would be. The United States Congress passed a series of laws designed to transfer cases from state courts to federal courts. In 1872, some of Youngsville's most prominent citizens were arrested.[127] They were indicted and charged "with a conspiracy to deprive citizens of rights guaranteed by the Constitution." All charges were dropped except those against Reuben Griffin Young, John D. Young, Ringgold Young and Neil Harkins. They were sentenced to ten years in federal prison, except Ringgold Young, who received a seven-year sentence and a $3,000 fine. The convicted men were marched through the streets of Montgomery as spectacles of their deeds as Klansmen; then they were transported to the New York Penitentiary in Albany. Their sentences were not completely served; the length of each was not recorded.

The textile mills were the economic center of the community. The pay that was earned at the mill typically was spent in the town, strengthening downtown businesses and organizations. In the early years of the mills' hiring, children were employed and worked alongside their parents and other family members. Child labor and convict labor were two of the most egregious practices of the early 1900s. The threat of unions, perhaps more than the actual unions, brought about amenities that workers enjoyed and remembered for the rest of their lives. They bonded with others at work, community functions, schools and sports.

Pursell Farms makes the connection between the past and present in the Talladega Springs story. The hallway in the inn is lined with pictures of the Old Talladega resort. Talladega's story is told in pictures of the glamorous days of the town. With the Talladega Mountains in the distance and the luxurious FarmLinks golf course, the inn appeals to new generations.

Each industry—the winemaking, the gold hunting that began with early explorers like de Soto—promised wealth that inspired the enterprising individuals who worked to achieve success in each business. No large repository of information about gold mining exists except geological reports and family stories captured in a few websites and essays. *Alabama Gold: A History of the South's Last Mother Lode* by this author was published by The History Press in July 2016. The book covers a century of gold mining activity in Alabama, from the 1830s intermittently through the Depression years in the 1930s. Recreational mining continues to take place in the Hillabee Creek and other areas.

The towns' stories are shared in state and national parks like Tannehill State Park in Tuscaloosa County. The park is included in the National Register of Historic Places. Other state and federal parks include Horseshoe Bend National Military Park, a 2,040-acre site of the last battle of the Creeks against Andrew Jackson; De Soto Caverns; and a U.S. national military park managed by the National Park Service that is the site of the last battle of the Creek. Each county and town library holds a treasure-trove of stories about the town. Comer Memorial Museum houses a treasure of Sylacauga marble sculptures and history and sponsors an annual marble festival.

Families labored together in the cotton fields, textile mills, coal mines, gold mines and any other money-producing industry at the time. The stories of individual towns present in varying degrees an overview of Alabama's struggle to be a prosperous state. The difficult days of laboring in cotton fields transitioned into cotton mill work, manufacturing jobs and work in technical fields. From the Depression days in the 1930s to financial prosperity following World War II to the closing of industries in the late twentieth century, the job market offered fewer opportunities. The stories of the Central Alabama ghost towns are inspiring, beautiful and equally awful as people awakened from dreams and lived the harsh realities of life. They created memories we treasure not always because of their successes but because they were our past, for the lives they lived and the legacy they passed to us.

NOTES

Preface

1. Windham, *Alabama*.

Chapter 1

2. Pickett, *History of Alabama*, 28.
3. Hudson, *Knights of Spain, Warriors of the Sun*, 248.
4. Ibid., 243.
5. Weddle, "European Exploration and Colonial Period."
6. PBS, "Story of…Smallpox."
7. McSween, "History of Childersburg."
8. Jensen, "Battle of Horseshoe Bend."
9. East, "War of 1812."
10. Robert Grierson was licensed as a trader in the Creek Nation. He was Alabama's lone Revolutionary War soldier. His great-grandson George Washington served as speaker of his nation in Oklahoma and Washington. He lived in the upper waters of Tallapoosa in present Clay County at Hillabee. *Alabama Historical Quarterly* (Winter 1944): 575; information submitted by Robert Grierson Chapter, DAR, Mrs. G.D. Halstead, Regent.
11. Abrams, "Cherokees in Alabama."

12. Abrams, "Tragedy of the Creek War."
13. Brigadier General James White in a report to his commander, Major General John Cocke, November 24, 1813, Encyclopedia of Alabama.
14. *Nashville Whig*, December 7, 1813; Jensen, "Battle of Horseshoe Bend."
15. *Nashville Whig*, December 7, 1813.
16. National Park Service, "Horseshoe Bend."
17. Alexander, "Battle of Horseshoe Bend."
18. Pickett, *History of Alabama*, 244–45.
19. Encyclopedia of Alabama, "Red Eagle."
20. National Park Service, "Survey of Historic Sites and Buildings."
21. Pickett, "Americans in Alabama and Mississippi," 299.
22. Jensen, "Battle of Horseshoe Bend."
23. National Park Service, "Major Participants."
24. Penick, "I Will Stamp Down My Foot."
25. Saxon, *Tallapoosa County*.
26. National Park Service, "Major Participants."

Chapter 2

27. Hutton, "Crockett and the Creek War."
28. Lewis, "Old St. Stephens."
29. Ibid., 18.
30. Ibid., 20.
31. Ibid., 25.
32. Mellown, "Steamboats in Alabama."
33. Lewis, *Lost Capitals of Alabama*, 20.
34. Lazenby, *History of Methodism in Alabama.*
35. Lewis, "Old St. Stephens."
36. Fairley, "Lost Capitals of St. Stephens and Cahawba," 23.
37. Alabama Historical Commission, "Just Beneath the Surface."
38. Fairley, "Lost Capitals of St. Stephens and Cahawba," 6.
39. Alabama Historical Commission, "Just Beneath the Surface."
40. Fry, "Memories of Old Cahaba."
41. Lewis, "Lafayette's Visit to Alabama."
42. Windham, *Alabama: One Big Front Porch*, ch. 4; Windham, *13 Alabama Ghosts and Jeffrey*, "Specter in the Maze at Cahaba."
43. Windham, *13 Alabama Ghosts*, 41.
44. Explore Rural SW Alabama, "Perine Well."
45. Old Cahawba, "Cahaba Federal Prison."

46. Old Cahawba, "Pegue's Ghost."
47. Digital Alabama, "Ghost of Sturdivant Hall."
48. Old Cahawba, "*Sultana* Tragedy."
49. Greer, "Sturdivant Hall Museum."
50. Old Cahawba, "Pegue's Ghost."
51. Old Cahawba, "Cahawba in the 1800s."
52. Cahaba River Society, "About the Cahaba River."
53. Nijhuis, "Cahaba: A River of Riches."

Chapter 3

54. Dean, "Golden Harvest of the Piedmont," 23–24.
55. Harris, *Dead Towns of Alabama*, 59.
56. Garner, "Gold Production in Alabama."
57. State of Alabama, National Register.
58. Phillips, "Preliminary Report on a Part of the Lower Gold Belt of Alabama," 3, 97.
59. Ibid., 41.
60. Coley, "Climax of Gold Mining."
61. Digital Alabama, "Gold in Coosa County."
62. Ibid.
63. Goggans, *Heritage of Coosa County*, 11.
64. Armes, *Story of Coal and Iron in Alabama*.
65. Ibid.
66. Bennett, "Tannehill Ironworks."
67. Ward, "Banner Mine Tragedy."
68. Greer, "Aldrich Coal Mining Museum."
69. "Alabama Mines."
70. Ghost Hunters Explore Sloss Furnace.
71. Cook, "Mining Alabama's Carrara."
72. Cook, *Magic in Stone*.
73. Berntson, "Vulcan State and Vulcan Park."
74. Visit Vulcan, "History."
75. Berntson, "Vulcan State and Vulcan Park."
76. AL Life and Culture, "Unique AL Monument Honors Woman Struck by Meteor.p."
77. Alabama Legacy, "DeSoto Caverns."
78. Alabama State Parks, "Cheaha State Park."

79. Ress, "De Soto Caverns."
80. Jemison, "Sketch of Talladega County."
81. Pursell Farms, "History of Talladega Springs."
82. Jemison, *Historic Tales of Talladega*, 1–3.

Chapter 4

83. Pursell Farms, "History of Talladega Springs."
84. Ibid.
85. Pursell Farms, "Four Generations."
86. Ibid.
87. Ibid.
88. Sulzby, *Historic Alabama Hotels and Resorts*.
89. Scott, "Clairmont Springs."
90. Cleburne County Chamber of Commerce, "History of Cleburne County."
91. Kaetz, "Fruithurst."
92. Stanton, "Fruithurst," 30–31.
93. O'Dell, *Images of America: Calhoun County*.
94. Ibid.

Chapter 5

95. Atkins, "Alabama Power Company."
96. Tharpe, "Lay Dam and Lake."
97. Cole, personal interview.
98. Atkins, "Lake Martin and the Thomas Wesley Martin Dam."
99. *St. Clair News-Aegis*, June 13, 1963.
100. Smith, "Remember Avondale Lake."
101. Sznajderman, "William Benson and the Kowaliga School," 22–29.
102. Library of Congress, "Tuskegee Institute."
103. Saxon, "Rural Communities," 141–42.
104. Russell, "History of Benjamin Russell and Russell Lands."

Chapter 6

105. Fickle, "Forest Products Industry in Alabama."
106. Walls, "Hillwood."

Chapter 7

107. Saxon, "Textile Giants," 176.
108. Russell, personal interview.
109. Walls and Oliver, *Images of America: Alexander City*.
110. Ibid.
111. Walls, *Alabama Gold*, 159.
112. Walls and Oliver, *Images of America: Alexander City*, 60.
113. McWhorter, "Avondale."
114. Textile World, "Avondale Closes Doors."
115. Ibid.
116. McWhorter, "Avondale."
117. National Park Service, National Register of Historic Places Program, "Pepperell Mill and Mill Village."
118. Ibid.
119. Cipperly, "History of Pepperell Mill."
120. Fry, "Ongoing Relevance of Norma Rae."
121. Montgomery Real-Time News, "Opelika's Pepperell Mill and Village."
122. Brook, "Old Cotton Mill in Tallassee."
123. Ibid.
124. Saxon, *Tallapoosa County*, 125, 129.
125. Goss, "History of Tallassee."
126. Haas, "Historic Tallassee Pre–Civil War Mill."

Afterword

127. Saxon, *Tallapoosa County*, 18.

BIBLIOGRAPHY

Abrams, Susan. "Cherokees in Alabama." Encyclopedia of Alabama. encyclopediaofalabama.org/article/h-1087.

———. "A Tragedy of the Creek War of 1813–1814." History Southeast. historysoutheast.com/hillabee.

Alabama Historical Commission. "Just Beneath the Surface." June 2, 2017. ahc.alabama.gov/news_detail.aspx?ID=12312.

Alabama Legacy. "DeSoto Caverns." Central Alabama, March 2017. www.alabamalegacy.org/desoto-caverns.

"Alabama Mines." www.miningartifacts.org/AlabamaMines.html.

Alabama State Parks. "Cheaha State Park." www.stateparks.com/cheaha_state_park_in_alabama.html.

Alexander, David. "Battle of Horseshoe Bend, Alabama." Legends of America. https://www.legendsofamerica.com/na-horseshoebend.

AL Life and Culture. "Unique AL Monument Honors Woman Struck by Meteor. September 29, 2020. www.al.com/life/2020/09/unique-alabama-monument-honors-woman-struck-by-meteor.html.

Armes, Ethel. *The Story of Coal and Iron in Alabama*. N.p., 1910. Repr., New York: Arno Press, 1973.

Atkins, Leah Rawls. "Alabama Power Company." Encyclopedia of Alabama. www.encyclopediaofalabama.org/article/h-1524.

———. "Lake Martin and the Thomas Wesley Martin Dam." Encyclopedia of Alabama. encyclopediaofalabama.org/article/h-1190.

Bennett, James R. "Tannehill Ironworks." Encyclopedia of Alabama. www.encyclopediaofalabama.org/article/h-1616.

Berntson, Ben. "Vulcan State and Vulcan Park." Encyclopedia of Alabama. encyclopediaofalabama.org/article/h-1557.

Brook, Ginger Ann. "Old Cotton Mill in Tallassee." Encyclopedia of Alabama. www.encyclopediaofalabama.org/article/m-3381.

Cahaba River Society. "About the Cahaba River." cahabariversociety.org/about-the-cahaba-river/#:~:text=The%20Cahaba%20River%20is%20Alabama's,in%20the%20Birmingham%20metro%20area.

Cipperly, Ann. "The History of Pepperell Mill." Opelika Observer, May 2, 2018. opelikaobserver.com/the-history-of-pepperell-mill.

Cleburne County Chamber of Commerce. "The History of Cleburne County." cleburnecountychamber.com/living-here.

Cole, Barbara. Personal interview, March 2019.

Coley, Judge C.J. "The Climax of Gold Mining." Lecture, AHA State Conference, Mobile, AL, May 5, 1967.

Cook, Ruth Beaumont. *Magic in Stone*. N.p., 2019.

———. "Mining Alabama's Carrara: The Forgotten History of Sylacauga's Marble Industry." *Alabama Heritage* 103 (Winter 2012).

Dean, Lewis. "Golden Harvest of the Piedmont." *Alabama Heritage*, 23–24.

Digital Alabama. "Ghost of Sturdivant Hall Walks the Halls at Night." digitalalabama.com/alabama-ghosts-and-haunted-places/ghost-of-sturdivant-hall-walks-the-halls-at-night/36993.

———. "Gold in Coosa County." digitalalabama.com/gold-in-alabama/gold-in-coosa-county-alabama/29469.

East, Don C. "The War of 1812 in Clay County." alabamaclaycounty.com/wp-content/uploads/2013/05/THE-WAR-OF-1812-IN-CLAY-COUNTY.pdf.

Encyclopedia of Alabama. "Red Eagle: Poem of the South." Courtesy of University of Alabama W.S. Hoole Special Collections Library. eoa.auburn.edu/article/m-2404.

Explore Rural SW Alabama. "Perine Well at the Old Cahawba Park Near Selma, AL." www.ruralswalabama.org/attraction/perine-well-old-cahawba-park.

Fairley, Nan. "The Lost Capitals of St. Stephens and Cahawba." *Alabama Heritage* 48 (Spring 1998): 26.

Fickle, James E. "Forest Products Industry in Alabama." Encyclopedia of Alabama, May 24, 2017. http://www.encyclopediaofalabama.org/article/h-3021.

Freepages. "Borden-Wheeler Springs Resort." freepages.rootsweb.com/~bkivak/genealogy/bordenspringshotel.htm.

Fry, Anna M. Gayle. "Memories of Old Cahaba." 1908. Trans. by Vicki Bryan. genealogytrails.com/ala/dallas/oldcahaba.html.

Fry, Naomi. "The Ongoing Relevance of Norma Rae." *New Yorker*, August 4, 2020. www.newyorker.com/recommends/watch/the-ongoing-relevance-of-norma-rae.

Garner, George. "Gold Production in Alabama." Encyclopedia of Alabama. encyclopediaofalabama.org/article/h-1666.

Ghost Hunters Explore Sloss Furnace. www.frightfurnace.com/ghost-hunters-explore-sloss-furnace.

Goggans, Dr. Mary Moss. *Heritage of Coosa County, Alabama*. N.p.: Heritage Publishing Consultants, 1999.

Goss, William E. (Bill). "A History of Tallassee." www.tallasseeal.gov/history-of-tallassee.

Greer, Carolyn. "Aldrich Coal Mining Museum." Encyclopedia of Alabama. encyclopediaofalabama.org/article/h-4159.

———. "Sturdivant Hall Museum." Encyclopedia of Alabama. encyclopediaofalabama.org/article/h-4190.

Haas, Katherine. "Historic Tallassee Pre–Civil War Mill a 'Total Loss' After Overnight Fire." *Opelika-Auburn News*, May 5, 2016. oanow.com/news/local/updated-historic-tallassee-pre-civil-war-mill-a-total-loss-after-overnight-fire/article_1dd87210-12dd-11e6-be65-1b90e53d760c.html.

Harris, Stuart. *Dead Towns of Alabama*. Tuscaloosa: University of Alabama Press, 1977.

Hudson, Charles. *Knights of Spain, Warriors of the Sun*. Athens: University of Georgia Press, 1997.

Hutton, Paul Andrew. "Crockett and the Creek War: 'We Now Shot Them Like Dogs.'" HistoryNet, December 2019. www.historynet.com/crockett-and-the-creek-war-we-now-shot-them-like-dogs.htm.

Jemison, E. Grace. "Sketch of Talladega County." In *Historic Tales of Talladega*. Montgomery, AL: Paragon Press, 1959.

Jensen, Ove. "Battle of Horseshoe Bend." Encyclopedia of Alabama. www.encyclopediaofalabama.org/article/h-1044.

Kaetz, James P. "Fruithurst." Encyclopedia of Alabama. www.encyclopediaofalabama.org/article/h-3779.

Lazenby, Marion Elias. *History of Methodism in Alabama and West Florida: Being an Account of the Amazing March of Methodism through Alabama and West Florida*. www.worldcat.org/title/history-of-methodism-in-alabama-and-west-florida-being-an-account-of-the-amazing-march-of-methodism-through-alabama-and-west-florida/oclc/1632564.

Lewis, Herbert J. "Daniel Pratt." Encyclopedia of Alabama. encyclopediaofalabama.org/article/h-1184.

———. "Lafayette's Visit to Alabama." Encyclopedia of Alabama. encyclopediaofalabama.org/article/h-2152.

———. *Lost Capitals of Alabama*. Charleston, SC: The History Press, 2014.

———. "Old St. Stephens." Encyclopedia of Alabama. encyclopediaofalabama.org/article/h-1674.

Library of Congress. "Tuskegee Institute—Training Leaders." African American Odyssey. www.loc.gov/exhibits/odyssey/educate/bookert.html.

McSween, Judy M. "History of Childersburg." www.childersburg.org/childersburghistory.shtml.

McWhorter, Price L. "Avondale." Encyclopedia of Alabama. encyclopediaofalabama.org/article/h-2141.

Mellown, Robert O. "Steamboats in Alabama." Encyclopedia of Alabama. www.encyclopediaofalabama.org/article/h-1803.

Montgomery Real-Time News. "Opelika's Pepperell Mill and Village Now on the National Register of Historic Places; See Images of Community." January 13, 2019. www.al.com/news/montgomery/2014/06/opelikas_pepperell_mill_and_vi.html.

Nashville Whig, December 7, 1813.

National Park Service. "Horseshoe Bend." www.nps.gov/hobe/learn/historyculture/major-participants-in-the-creek-war.htm.

———. "Major Participants in the Creek War." www.nps.gov/hobe/learn/historyculture/major-participants-in-the-creek-war.htm.

———. "Survey of Historic Sites and Buildings." www.nps.gov/parkhistory/online_books/founders/sitec2.htm.

National Park Service, National Register of Historic Places Program. "The Pepperell Mill and Mill Village Historic District." www.nps.gov/nr/feature/places/14000090.htm.

Nijhuis, Michelle. "The Cahaba: A River of Riches." *Smithsonian Mag*, August 2009. www.smithsonianmag.com/science-nature/the-cahaba-a-river-of-riches-34214889.

O'Dell, Kimberly. *Images of America: Calhoun County*. Charleston, SC: Arcadia Publishing, 1998.

Old Cahawba. "Cahaba Federal Prison." cahawba.com/history-and-legacy/cahaba-federal-prison.

———. "Cahawba in the 1800s." cahawba.com/history-and-legacy/cahawba-in-the-1800s.

———. "Pegue's Ghost." cahawba.com/history-and-legacy/pegues-ghost.

———. "The *Sultana* Tragedy." cahawba.com/history-and-legacy/the-sultana-tragedy.

PBS. "The Story of…Smallpox—And Other Deadly Eurasian Germs." Variables. www.pbs.org/gunsgermssteel/variables/smallpox.html.

Penick, James, Jr. "I Will Stamp Down My Foot and Shake Down Every House." *American Heritage* 27, no. 1 (December 1975). www.americanheritage.com/i-will-stamp-ground-my-foot-and-shake-down-every-house#4.

Phillips, W.B. "A Preliminary Report on a Part of the Lower Gold Belt of Alabama in the Counties of Chilton, Coosa, and Tallapoosa." *Alabama Geological Survey Bulletin* 3, no. 97 (1892).

Pickett, Albert James. "The Americans in Alabama and Mississippi." In *History of Alabama: And Incidentally of Georgia and Mississippi from the Earliest Period.* Vol. 2. quod.lib.umich.edu/m/moa/AFJ9604.0001.001?rgn=main;view=fulltext.

Pursell Farms. "Four Generations of Family Business and Alabama Heritage." pursellfarms.com/about-us/history.

———. "History of Talladega Springs." pursellfarms.com/talladega-springs.

———. "The Pursell Family." pursellfarms.com/about-us/pursell-family.

Ress, Thomas V. "De Soto Caverns." Encyclopedia of Alabama, March 28, 2012. www.encyclopediaofalabama.org/article/h-3243.

Russell, Ben. "The History of Benjamin Russell and Russell Lands, Inc." July 7, 2009. benrussell.com/Ben-history%20of%20Russell%20Lands.htm.

———. Personal interview, 2016, Russell Lands.

Saxon, Bob, ed. Brigadier General James White in a report to his commander, Major General John Cocke. In *Tallapoosa County, a History.* Alexander City, AL: Tallapoosa County Bicentennial Committee, 1976.

———. "Rural Communities, the West Side of the River." In *Tallapoosa County, a History.* Alexander City, AL: Tallapoosa County Bicentennial Committee, 1976.

Scott, John. "Clairmont Springs." *Alabama Heritage* 42 (Fall 1966).

Smith, Jerry C. "Remember Avondale Lake." Logan Martin Lake. www.loganmartinlakelife.com/remember-avondale-lake.

Stanton, Mary. "Fruithurst: The Alabama Wine Country." *Alabama Heritage* (Spring 2009): 30–31.

State of Alabama. National Register. ahc.alabama.gov/Alabama%20Register%20Properties/Cleburne%20County/AL.CleburneCounty.ArbacoocheeOCR.pdf.

St. Clair News-Aegis, June 13, 1963.

Sulzby, James F. *Historic Alabama Hotels and Resorts*. Tuscaloosa: University of Alabama Press, 1960.

Sznajderman, Michael Atkins. "William Benson and the Kowaliga School." *Alabama Heritage* (Spring 2005): 22–29.

Textile World. "Avondale Closes Doors Sells Some Facilities." July 23, 2006. www.textileworld.com/textile-world/textile-news/2006/07/avondale-mills-closes-doors-sells-some-facilities.

Tharpe, Bill. "Lay Dam and Lake." Encyclopedia of Alabama. encyclopediaofalabama.org/article/h-1904.

Visit Vulcan. "History." visitvulcan.com/about/timeline/#:~:text=Vulcan%20is%20dedicated%20at%20the,Moretti%20also%20won%20a%20medal.

Walls, Peggy J. *Alabama Gold: A History of the South's Last Mother Lode*. Charleston, SC: The History Press, 2016.

———. "Hillwood." *Coosa County News*, n.d.

Walls, Peggy J., and Laura B. Oliver. *Images of America: Alexander City*. Charleston, SC: Arcadia Publishing, 2016.

Ward, Robert David. "Banner Mine Tragedy of 1911." Encyclopedia of Alabama, April 22, 2020. encyclopediaofalabama.org/article/h-1135.

Weddle, Robert S. "European Exploration and Colonial Period." Encyclopedia of Alabama, April 1, 2014. www.encyclopediaofalabama.org/article/h-1180.

Windham, Kathryn Tucker. *Alabama: One Big Front Porch*. N.p.: Strode Publishers, Inc., 1975.

———. "The Specter in the Maze at Cahaba." In *13 Alabama Ghosts and Jeffrey*. N.p., n.d.

ABOUT THE AUTHOR

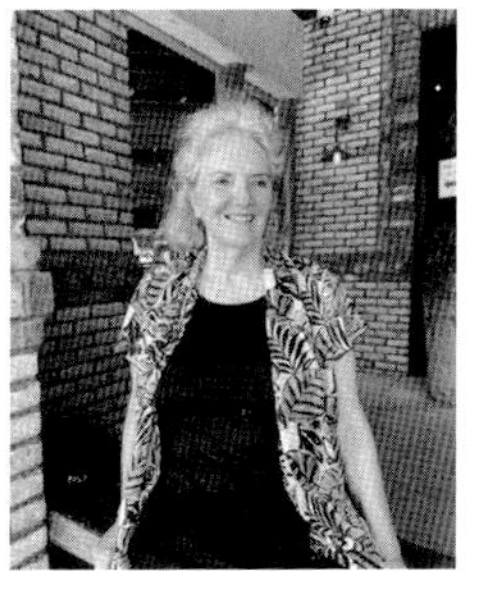

Peggy Walls is a retired English and communications instructor at Benjamin Russell High School, Central Alabama Community College and Auburn University and an online instructor for the University of Phoenix. She is a member of historical, lineage and writing societies, including the Tohopeka Chapter of the Daughters of the American Revolution, Alabama Historical Association, Tallapoosee Historical Society, Alabama Writers' Forum, National League of American Penwomen, Alabama's Writers Conclave and the Alabama State Poetry Association. She earned an undergraduate degree in secondary education from Auburn University at Montgomery and a master of arts degree and postgraduate professional educators certification from Auburn University. Her interests are history and lineage research, poetry and art. She is the author of *Alabama Gold: A History of the South's Last Mother Lode* and articles published in *Alabama Review* and *Alabama Heritage*, plus multiple news articles. She enjoys spending time with her family.